Studies on Revelatio

MW00895852

SHOW
AND
TELL

How God Reveals Truth to Us

Leo R. Van Dolson, Ph.D.

Pacific Press® Publishing Association
Nampa, Idaho
Oshawa, Ontario, Canada

Edited by Kenneth R. Wade
Designed by Dennis Ferree
Cover art by Lars Justinen

Copyright © 1998 by
Pacific Press® Publishing Association
Printed in the United States of America
All Rights Reserved

ISBN 0-8163-1681-3

98 99 00 01 02 • 5 4 3 2 1

Contents

Introduction

Because it is impossible for human minds to discover what we need to know about God, He shows (through revelation) and tells (through inspiration) everything that we can grasp about His infinite nature and infinite goodness. The fullest and clearest revelation of God is found in His Written Word, the Bible, and in the Living Word, Jesus.

Satan is doing everything he can today to make human beings skeptical of and disinterested in God's revelations. He uses what is termed "science" to lead people to think that only that which is reasonable to sin-perverted human minds is true. Thus human intelligence becomes the arbiter of whether the revelations of God are correct. Consequently, humans have rejected basically every aspect of God's self-revelation.

A good deal of time and space could be given in this book to dealing with the questions and objections raised by the skeptics and those who have distorted the truth on this subject. Instead, the approach taken here focuses on reviewing the clear and positive information God has given concerning understanding His revealed will. The positive approach alone can provide us with the truth we need to thwart the continuing attacks and distortions of Satan who can raise more questions than we have time to answer.

Thus, this book does not name the names of those holding contrary views.   Others have done that.   Instead, I have attempted to deal with issues in the way Jesus did. The following Ellen White counsel helped me find a way to deal with divergent views without pinpointing the individuals who are teaching them:

> The trials of the children of Israel, and their attitude just before the first coming of Christ, have been presented before me again and again to illustrate the position of the people of God in their experience before the second coming of Christ— how the enemy sought every occasion to take control of the minds of the Jews, and today he is seeking to blind the minds of God's servants, that they may not be able to discern the precious truth (*Selected Messages*, 1:406).

By showing how Jesus met the same questions we face today, we answer the critics without having to identify them by name. At the end of each chapter you will find a section on how Jesus met His critics with simple truth that exposed their false teachings.

In this final show and tell time our challenge is to develop a close, trusting relationship with the Lord. When we do this, we take Him at His word. Then the inspired writings He gave to help us understand His revelations will be reflected in our lives and in a unified teaching based on what God shows us and tells us. In that way we, as reflectors of Christ, will join in His mission of showing and telling it to the world.

Chapter 1

GOOD GOD—GOOD BOOK

It took a good God to produce the Good Book!

One of the first prayers many children learn is the "grace" whose first lines read:

> "God is great, God is good.
> Let us thank Him for this food. . . ."

Often it seems easier for us to understand how *great* God is than how *good* He is. We think of Him in the highest heaven as being omnipotent, omnipresent, and omniscient and sing "How great Thou art!" But it also is essential for us as growing Christians to contemplate how GOOD God is. Particularly today when Satan has launched an all-out attack to convince the world that God is anything but good. At times of stress even some Christians doubt God's goodness. One of Satan's most subtle attacks in this scientific age is through the so-called theory of evolution that contradicts God's loving involvement in the development of our world and in providing sustaining care for His creation.

Science is at its best when it deals with events that are happening right now, or at least can be made to happen now. But when we get into the area of the origin of matter and life, we go beyond the limits of the scientific method.

Some scientists act as though the discussion that has raged for more than one hundred years between those who accept the hypothesis of evolution and those who accept the Bible record of special creation was settled long ago in favor of evolution. But that is not so. There is not adequate evidence on either side to prove one position or the other scientifically and conclusively. The Bible teaching of specific creation is outside the province and scope of science, but it is not internally unscientific. The evolutionary hypothesis, on the other hand, contradicts such scientific laws as the second law of thermodynamics (the general natural tendency to go from order to disorder) and the law of probability (the chance of life evolving on earth in five billion years is one out of one followed by 40,000 zeroes).

In the long run, the choice between which theory of origins we accept boils down to the question of basic assumptions. Here creationists have the advantage. The Bible record of the creation of life comes from the Creator Himself. He *was* there. He made it happen.

For those biased by the assumptions they have been taught, it is difficult to listen to what God has to say about how He made the worlds. We need to have our ears so attuned to the voice of God that we are willing to listen when He tells us through such representatives as the prophet Isaiah, "the Lord thy maker, . . . hath stretched forth the heavens, and laid the foundations of the earth" (Isa. 51:13, KJV); and the prophet Jeremiah who adds: "He hath made the earth by his power, he hath established the world by his wisdom, and hath stretched out the heavens by his discretion" (Jer. 10:12).

When we accept the Bible as our guide to understanding the natural world, we find nature pointing to a *good* Creator. Ellen White tells us that "In His teaching from nature, Christ was speaking of the things which His own hands had made, and which had qualities and powers that He Himself had imparted. In their original perfection all created things were an expression of the thought of God. . . . The earth is now marred and defiled by sin. Yet even in its blighted state much that is beautiful remains. God's object lessons are not obliterated; rightly understood, nature speaks of her Creator" (*Christ's Object Lessons*, 18).

Scripture and Science

After stating that the Creator can be "clearly seen, being understood by the things that are made" (Rom. 1:20), the apostle Paul suggests that "professing themselves to be wise" so many have become "fools" instead, because they "changed the glory of the uncorruptible God into an image made like to corruptible man, and to birds, and fourfooted beasts, and creeping things" (verses 22, 23).

The apostle's words can be applied not only to the custom of idolatry current in his day but also to a philosophy that even then was being given credence in some circles—the concept that life evolved from simple forms into the many complex forms that now exist. Paul suggests that it is absurd to degrade God to the image of created beings. Why? A partial answer lies in the fact that humans are not always dependable. We are changeable and often capricious, just as were the ancient gods symbolized by the idols about which Paul was concerned. When we make our Father in heaven that kind of god we are forced, in turn, to adopt the concept that there can be no absolute law, order, or harmony in the universe. However, science itself is based on the one essential presupposition that there are dependable laws that govern life as we know it.

As seen in the book of Job, the Bible develops the concept of a great, intelligent Designer who alone can put together the complicated factors that must be present for a particular organism to function. Evolutionists who assume that improbable events can happen given eons of time, recently have had the tables turned on them by biochemist Michael Behe, who demonstrates that supposed evolutionary events that have practically zero probability of occurring become even *less* likely given *more* time.

Behe's *Darwin's Black Box*[1] challenges Darwin's statement in *The Origin of Species* that if any complex organ existed that could not possibly have been formed by numerous successive slight modifications, his theory would absolutely break down. Behe's challenge to Darwin revolves around the fact that to Darwin the cell was a "black box" whose inner workings were a complete mystery. But now we have a much better idea of how cells work and can show that a multitude of discoveries in the ultracomplex world of molecular machinery and cellular systems over the past forty years indicate that Darwin's theories have broken down absolutely. It is a fact that such complex systems as human vision, blood coagulation, and immunity could not have developed by chance.

Behe refers to systems that have "irreducible complexity" as being unable to evolve. In his lectures, he flashes on the screen a diagram of a simple mousetrap. Pointing out the five components necessary for a mousetrap to function, he states that you need all five parts functioning at one time in order to catch a mouse. You can't catch a few mice with a plain wooden platform and then add a spring and catch a few more. All parts must be present and in working order if the trap is to function. The mousetrap is irreducibly complex. As scientists explore the interior of a cell, evidence faces them that the systems were directly designed by an intelligent agent.

Over the last fifteen or twenty years several other major scientific discoveries have challenged Darwinism. Take, for instance, the geneticists' current understanding of the double-helixed DNA molecule. It is now thought that the messages sent by the genetic code are dependent upon the specific sequences of nucleotides in the DNA molecule rather than upon the properties of the nucleotide constituents themselves. Chemist Charles Thaxton states that this "so-called 'information problem' of genetics . . . poses the most serious threat to naturalistic explanations about the origin of life" (Charles Thaxton, "Theoretical Clay Feet," *Eternity*, Sept. 1985, 16). To think that amino acids could arrange themselves into such a complex information system by themselves is beyond belief. Such a clever and complicated design must have a Designer.

The highly plausible alternative to the evolutionary hypothesis is the Bible record of special creation. But that, too, takes faith to accept. "Through faith we understand that the worlds were framed by the word of God, so that things which are seen were not made of things which do appear" (Heb. 11:3). In the creation of the world, God was not dependent upon preexisting matter. By divine fiat the world was created out of nothing.

The advent of nuclear science has made it possible to understand to a limited degree how the power of God could be transformed into the matter needed to bring our world into existence. The energy released in a nuclear explosion testifies to the tremendous amount of power and energy it took to put the atoms together in the beginning.

The first human beings, Adam and Eve, were made in the image of God as the crowning work of Creation (Gen. 1:26). God gave them dominion over the earth and charged them with the responsibility to care for it (Gen. 1:27-30). When the work of Creation was finished, God declared that it was "very good" (Gen. 1:31). God brought order to the earth's surface and created all plant and animal life in six literal twenty-four-hour days. All of this is in direct conflict with the hypothesis of evolution.

The Greatest Evidence

Julian Huxley, in his book *Man Stands Alone*, pictures the human race as a curious byproduct of a universe utterly indifferent to life. This bleak thought—the natural outgrowth of the evolutionistic-humanistic teaching—has led to the fear, hopelessness, and despair that characterize many today.

Ever since the nuclear age began at Hiroshima, we have lived in a perpetual crisis atmosphere so terrifying, so universal, and so altogether unprecedented that it has numbed hopes for the future. The twentieth century, which was touted back in the thirties as the "Century of Progress," more than met its promise technologically. What, then, has taken the golden sheen from our age of promise, progress, and plenty? Human beings, children of the eternal God, have proclaimed themselves as the sons and daughters of Mother Mud. Evolution and humanism can lead only to fear, frustration, and despair, because humanity cannot lift itself out of the mire of sin by its own bootstraps.

The greatest evidence of what is wrong with the theory of evolution is seen in the results of its circulation for more than one hundred fifty years. Mother Mud is linked inevitably with Father Fear. But it does not end there. Many years ago some perceptive college youth recognized the implications of the theory of evolution and organized an atheists' club on their campus that took as its slogan: "Sons of apes don't need a Saviour!"

A tremendous truth is involved in that slogan. Not only did God create this world, but His goodness, love, and benevolence also have been demonstrated ever since in the fact that He sustains all creation on a moment-by-moment basis. (See Col. 1:17; Heb. 1:3.) Even beyond that is His desire to carry on His relationship with the human beings He had created after their rebellion broke the harmony and destroyed the perfection that existed before the advent of sin. In spite of the disaster sin brought on the physical world and the changes for the worse in the nature of human beings, there still is enough design, order, and beauty in nature to help us understand the love of God for fallen beings.

However, the greatest evidence of God's goodness can be found in Christ's sacrifice at Calvary. The New Testament makes a point of the fact that Christ was our Creator. (See John 1:1-3, 14; Col. 1:13-17.) Therefore, it was our Maker Himself who gave His life on the cross that we might have eternal life. Our Creator became our Redeemer. He is able to create new hearts within us and to restore us to the privilege of being sons and daughters of God. (See Heb. 10:16, 17; 1 John 3:1, 2.) Life takes on meaning, and human existence takes on purpose only in the fact that our Creator became our Saviour. But if we were sons and daughters of apes or of primordial ooze, there would be no permanent values, and we would not need a Saviour. There is no way of reconciling these two opposite approaches to, or philosophies of, life.

Those who believe the Bible record of special creation see every display of creative and re-creative power on the part of God as evidence of His personal interest, love, and goodness. Not only is this reassuring, but it bodes well for the future. Where is the era of evolutionary science leading? Many believe it will end in nuclear destruction of the earth or in ecological disaster. Where does belief in a loving God who created us and has our best interest in view lead? To "new heavens and a new earth, wherein dwelleth righteousness" (2 Pet. 3:13). People who accept God as Creator and His plan for their lives find a more abundant life now as they cooperate with His plan for the present (see John 10:10) as well as an even more abundant eternity. When it comes to deciding on concepts of origins, we need to keep the future in mind. When you compare the prospects, there is no contest.

One of the reasons why human beings are prone to seek naturalistic explanations for their origin is that they are afraid of the implications involved in having to maintain a relationship with a Creator God. Therefore they tend to concentrate on what they point to as injustice and cruelty on God's part. They earnestly search the Bible looking for anything they can interpret this way. They look upon God's "demands" as being stifling to their development and feel that what He expresses as being best for them is contrary to all that interests them. They feel that God is trying to cheat them out of that which they consider desirable.

But if they would just give the God of Creation and the God of the Bible a chance to speak to them, they would soon learn that a truly good and loving God has only their best interests in mind and bends over backward to try to make life, even in a sinful world, as pleasant and hopeful as it can be. Because our good God loves us and is interested in every aspect of our lives, He has given the Bible to help us get the most out of life. It is a good God who created, redeemed, and sanctified those He has created. (Incidentally, all three of those aspects of His goodness just listed are memorialized in the institution of the Sabbath.) It is a good God whose heart is touched by the loss of even one sparrow, let alone by the tragic loss of one of His earthly children. It is a good God who generously provides our daily bread and everything else we need to sustain life. And this good and loving God wants us to know as much about Him as our human minds can possibly grasp. Therefore, He has gone to great lengths to reveal Himself, His love, and His goodness to us.

Our acceptance of what He reveals leads to a trust in Him that reaches out the hand of faith, takes Him at His Word, and accepts all the precious blessings He longs to share with us. Such faith can be defined in the way Ellen White explains it as "the assent of man's understanding to God's words, that binds the heart to God's service" (*Ye*

Shall Receive Power, 195).

There are those who choose to question and quibble over the revelations that a good and loving heavenly Father has provided. I choose not to. I am thrilled with whatever form or method the gracious God chooses to reveal Himself to us and to preserve His revelation over the centuries. I consider it a privilege to take His Word as He has given it to me and search out as best I can His wishes and His will in order to put them to work in my life.

Because He is a good God, I know that what He wants for me is far more beneficent and pleasurable than anything I can ever choose or find for myself. Let the critics quibble. I intend to spend my time and effort discovering the precious jewels of truth hidden in the Bible treasure chest, and I hope you will too. All the treasure of heaven is available to us in God's Word if we just reach out the hand of faith and accept it for ourselves.

How Jesus Revealed the Goodness of God

Nicodemus had a lot to think about after his nighttime interview with Jesus. As a strict Pharisee he shared the sect's misunderstanding of God and the plan of salvation. But as he watched Christ's actions and listened to His teachings, the Pharisee began to glimpse something wonderful existing beyond His limited vision of God's revelation. He pondered and studied. In a particular way, his attention was drawn by Christ to the symbol of the serpent in the wilderness. It helped him realize that God' love included Jesus' dying as One who bore our sins to provide our only means of salvation. Then the leading Pharisee stood beneath the cross, witnessing the scene Ellen White describes so movingly. "The spotless Son of God hung upon the cross, His flesh lacerated with stripes; those hands so often reached out in blessing, nailed to the wooden bars; those feet so tireless on ministries of love, spiked to the tree; that royal head pierced by the crown of thorns; those quivering lips shaped to the cry of woe. And all that He endured—the blood drops that flowed from His head, His hands, His feet, the agony that racked

His frame, and the unutterable anguish that filled His soul at the hiding of His Father's face—speaks to each child of humanity, declaring, It is for thee that the Son of God consents to bear this burden of guilt; for thee He spoils the domain of death, and opens the gates of Paradise. He who stilled the angry waves and walked the foam-capped billows, who made devils tremble and disease flee, who opened blind eyes and called forth the dead to life,— offers Himself upon the cross as a sacrifice, and this from love to thee. He, the Sin Bearer, endures the wrath of divine justice, and for thy sake becomes sin itself" (*The Desire of Ages,* 755, 756).

Probably at that moment Nicodemus understood what was taking place more clearly than any other human in his time. He yielded His life to the God of love and from that point on took an uncompromising stand for Christ and His church.

But the extent of God's love goes far beyond what Nicodemus understood at the time. Jesus did much more than restore humanity to what we were at Creation. "By His life and His death, Christ has achieved even more than recovery from the ruin wrought through sin. It was Satan's purpose to bring about an eternal separation between God and man; but in Christ we become more closely united to God than if we had never fallen. In taking our nature, the Saviour has bound Himself to humanity by a tie that is never to be broken. Through the eternal ages He is linked with us. 'God so loved the world, that He gave His only-begotten Son.' John 3:16. He gave Him not only to bear our sins, and to die as our sacrifice; He gave Him to the fallen race. To assure us of His immutable counsel of peace, God gave His only-begotten Son to become one of the human family, forever to retain His human nature.... God has adopted human nature in the person of His Son, and has carried the same into the highest heaven. It is the 'Son of man' who shares the throne of the universe. . . . In Christ the family of earth and the family of heaven are bound together. Christ glorified is our brother. Heaven is enshrined in humanity, and humanity is enfolded in the bosom of Infinite Love" (*The Desire of Ages,* 25, 26).

Actually, even now, none of us can appreciate how GOOD and loving our God is. But someday we will see and know.

---

1. Michael J. Behe, *Darwin's Black Box: The Biochemical Challenge to Evolution* (New York: Free Press, 1996).

Chapter 2

GOD WANTS US TO KNOW HIM

One of the rages that swept the United States in the seventies was proclaiming that God is dead. Woody Allen, who obviously had little knowledge about God, is quoted as saying "Not only is there no God, but try getting a plumber on weekends!" He probably was right about not being able to get a plumber on weekends in his locale but was definitely wrong about there being no God. Some college students of that era adopted the slogan, "God isn't dead—He just doesn't want to get involved." That was wrong too. The problem was and is that people weren't and aren't listening to God.

The God of the Bible is a God who reveals Himself to us. He does not leave us alone in our state of lostness, alienated from Him because of sin. He comes to us, showing us His character, revealing His will, offering us the salvation He has provided. The Bible came to us as God ordered it over a period of 1,600 years. But even the first words written were as relevant to the population of the world at the beginning of the third millennium A.D. as to those to whom it was first given—probably even more so. As God began communicating to Adam and Eve on the sixth day of Creation, He accepted the challenge of making what was being written meaningful to all who would live in a sin-filled world. Those who accuse God of an incomplete revelation overlook His ability to do that which no human could accomplish.

If eternal life comes through knowing God, as John 17:1-5 insists, and God offers us eternal life, then it is His responsibility to make it possible for us to know as much about Him as we need to know to have eternal life. Later we'll discuss what it means to really know Him. But first let's note what chapter 10 in *Steps to Christ* tells us about how the Lord has made it possible for us to know Him. The overall impression we get as we study this chapter is *how much He wants us to know and trust Him*!

Basically, *Steps to Christ* outlines four ways that God has given us of learning about Him:

1. God Speaks Through Nature

"The listening ear can hear and understand the communications of God through the things of nature. The green fields, the lofty trees, the buds and flowers, the passing cloud, the falling rain, the babbling brook, the glories of the heavens, speak to our hearts, and invite us to become acquainted with Him who made them all" (*Steps to Christ*, 84).

One of our problems as humans is that, ordinarily, we only hear what we want to hear. The fact that we can hear best what we most want to hear is illustrated by the experience of naturalist, Charles Kellogg. One day when he and a friend were walking down a street in New York City, Kellogg stopped, listened a moment, and said to his friend, "Do you hear that?"

"Hear what, Charlie?"

"That cricket singing?"

"What cricket? How can you hear a cricket in the midst of all the noises here in the city?

"Come," the naturalist replied. "Let me show you." He led his friend to a crack in a nearby wall. Sure enough, there was a cricket.

"Charlie, I still don't understand how you could hear a cricket in the midst of all the noise here in the city."

Kellogg took a dime out of his pocket and dropped it on the street. Several passersby turned around to look.

"You see," the naturalist said, "In the midst of all this noise those people could hear a dime drop. It depends on what you have your ears attuned to. Mine are attuned to the sounds of nature."

When the ears of our souls are attuned to the voice of God, we not only hear but respond as He seeks to teach us about Himself. "If we will but listen, God's created works will teach us precious lessons of obedience and trust" (ibid.).

Not only will Christians learn to trust God more as they recognize His loving care all about them, but they will be able to recognize more clearly how nature testifies of its Creator: "The poet and the naturalist have many things to say about nature, but it is the Christian who enjoys the beauty of the earth with the highest appreciation, because he recognizes his Father's handiwork and perceives His love in flower and shrub and tree. No one can fully appreciate the significance of hill and vale, river and sea, who does not look upon them as an expression of God's love to man" (ibid., 87).

2. God Speaks Through Providence

"God speaks to us through His providential workings and through the influence of His Spirit upon the heart. In our circumstances and surroundings, in the changes daily taking place around us, we may find precious lessons if our hearts are but open to discern them" (ibid., 87).

In this connection we need to consider two texts from the Psalms:

"He loveth righteousness and judgment: the earth is full of the goodness of the LORD" (Ps. 33:5).

"Whoso [is] *wise*, and will observe these [things], even

they shall *understand* the lovingkindness of the LORD"
(Ps. 107:43, italics supplied).

Unfortunately, we usually do not recognize Providence
at work for us until we get in some desperate circumstance
where we have to call on the Lord to help us. But God's
goodness leads us each day in many ways we often fail to
recognize or appreciate.

3. God Speaks Through His Word

"God speaks to us in His word. Here we have in clearer
lines the revelation of His character, of His dealings with men,
and the great work of redemption" (*Steps to Christ*, 87).

Thus the Scriptures point out that we can know God
and follow His will in the same way that people through
the ages have. The Scriptures provide spiritual food and
drink—our nurture: "Fill the whole heart with the words
of God. They are the living water, quenching your burning thirst. They are the living bread from heaven. . . . Our
bodies are built up from what we eat and drink; and as in
the natural economy, so in the spiritual economy: it is what
we meditate upon that will give tone and strength to our
spiritual nature" (ibid., 88). Spiritual *nature* depends on
spiritual *nurture*.

Try jumping to heaven from your backyard. How high
were you able to jump? There is no way we can make it to
heaven on our own. That is why God took the initiative
and came down to us. For revelation to be revelation it
must have supernatural quality. It comes as something
from outside our world. Not merely is it the product of
history. It does not spring from human creativity. It is a
message from beyond the human realm and therefore
comes to inform, motivate, and change us. In the same
way as Christ came into this world, divine thoughts have
come to this earth, born into the minds of prophets, who
gave them to us in human expression.

The Holy Spirit is able to preserve the divine within the human. In the same way that the divine and human natures were united in Jesus, divine thoughts were kept preserved by the Spirit within human expressions. Thus the Bible is at once fully human, but more than human. Through its human words, thoughts, patterns, ideas, concepts, and history, God speaks.

We cannot expect either the Bible or our Christian experience to be meaningful without daily feeding on God's Word. But once we learn to feed ourselves daily on the Bread of Life, we develop a *taste* for it and become *hungry* when we neglect it.

When you stop and analyze it carefully, you'll have to admit that the most likely reason why people do not like to study the Bible is because they find things there that cut across their desired way of living. But after all, that's the Bible's purpose, isn't it? The Bible wouldn't be much good to us if reading it didn't make us better people. The one thing we have to grasp is that *better isn't bitter*! God wants us to have the very best, the more abundant life.

When we realize that God's will for us, as expressed in His laws and requirements, is His special promise that He will enable us to get the very best out of life, our attitude toward the Bible should change drastically. Instead of ignoring God's requirements and hoping that they'll go away or somehow do not apply in our case, we'll long to search them out and take *joy and delight* in them.

How do we prevent *truth* decay? By brushing daily with the Bible *truth*brush! Such study results in our being so totally committed to God's will because of our love for Him that everything we do, say, or even think may be the *simple outworking of His will* for us.

That just naturally leads us to the fourth step in knowing God.

4. God Speaks Through the Character of Jesus

"The theme of redemption is one that the angels desire to look into; it will be the science and the song of the redeemed throughout the ceaseless ages of eternity. Is it not worthy of careful thought and study now?" (ibid., 88, 89).

Our salvation is the purpose of God's seeking. He wants us to know how we can be saved. Nothing about salvation has its origin on our side. It comes from His side. But it has been worked out on our side; coming to fruition or meaning. Christ came from heaven, was born into the human family, and worked out salvation within human history.

Matthew 13 pictures a pearl merchant as gladly selling the precious jewels he had accumulated during his lifetime in order to gain possession of the one spectacularly beautiful and precious pearl of great price. As we study the Bible, we need to keep in mind that the salvation offered through Jesus cannot be purchased by anything we do. We cannot earn it. It was blood-bought for us at Calvary by the sacrifice of God's own Son. There was and is no way that any of us could ever pay that kind of price.

What does it mean, then, for the merchantman to sell all that he had in order to buy the magnificent pearl? This is a beautiful representation of those who appreciate the truths of God's salvation so highly that they *joyfully, gladly* give up all they have in order to possess it.

Note that the price we pay is *not* the price of our salvation but *is* the price of our acceptance. Christ alone was able to pay the great price for salvation, but acceptance and surrender cost us everything we have. The pearl merchant who found the one great pearl gave up only what he had. We must be fully detached from self and sin if Christ is to have all there is of us.

It is Jesus who is the flawless Pearl of great price. In

Him is gathered all the lustrous glory and beauty of heaven. His purity and righteousness are as unstained as the beautiful white pearl. Every page of the Holy Scriptures shines with the light of the Pearl of great price. In comparison with His precious beauty of life and character, all else fades into insignificance.

We must find the Pearl of great price for ourselves. We must learn to know Jesus—not just know about Him but know Him as our personal Saviour from sin. It is of utmost importance to know what He would do with them if He had our hands and feet. We must learn what He would be thinking if He had taken over our minds. The way we learn this and come to know Him intimately for ourselves and identify fully with Him is through careful and consistent daily study of His life as revealed in the Bible.

The Holy Spirit as Our Guide and Counselor

Not only has God given us four ways of knowing Him, but He has given the Holy Spirit as our Guide and Counselor to make sure we get the message straight. The Holy Spirit guides us into all truth by helping us sort out truth from the counterfeit and misinformation with which Satan now floods our world. "All from the oldest to the youngest need to be taught of God. We may be taught by man to see the truth clearly, but God alone can teach the heart to receive the truth savingly, which means to receive the words of eternal life into good and honest hearts. The Lord is waiting patiently to instruct every willing soul who will be taught. The fault is not with the willing Instructor, the greatest Teacher the world ever knew, but it is with the learner who holds his own impressions and ideas, and will not give up his human theories and come in humility to be taught. He will not allow his conscience and his heart to be educated, disciplined, and trained. . . .

"Those who search the Scriptures, and most earnestly

seek to understand them, will reveal the sanctification of the Spirit through the belief of the truth, for they take into their very heart the truth, and have that faith that works by love and purifies the soul. All their spiritual sinew and muscle are nourished by the Bread of Life which they eat" (*Manuscript Releases*, 8:162, 163).

A Close Relationship With Jesus Is Essential to Understanding

Knowing God includes much more than intellectual understanding. It represents a continual, intimate, and close relationship that leads us to so trust Him that we accept His revealed way as the very best for us. Because we understand His great loving concern for us, we are more than willing to let Him take over and restructure our lives.

Yet, like the religious leaders of Jesus' day, we often pontificate on concepts beyond our ability to understand and argue over inconsequential points of theology, thus missing that which is the center and focus of Scripture. Isn't Jesus saying to us, "You diligently study the Scriptures because you think that by them you possess eternal life. These are the Scriptures that testify about me, yet you refuse to come to me to have life" (John 5:39, 40, NIV)? In our selfish pride we overlook that which is of such precious significance—the only reason Scriptures have been given us—the testimony of Jesus, the greatest gift imaginable.

How much we miss if we allow the pride of intellect to prevent our acceptance of His offer to bring us the more abundant life now and the unimaginable riches of eternal life! How dare we wander down the path of theological pride and intransigence when the purpose of His revelation is that we might develop such a close and loving relationship with Him that those about us will recognize His footsteps when we walk by?

I will never forget Dr. Floyd Bresee's simple but effective illustration of God's kind of love. He pictures a father calling the family together to see how Junior has learned to take his first steps. Grandpa, a few steps away, is smiling and encouraging Junior as father lets go of him. Junior takes one wobbly step, then another, then falls flat on his face. Floyd asked the Sabbath School class to which he was telling this story what the father's reaction would be. Would he turn red with embarrassment and yell at the would-be toddler, "What's the matter with you, you stupid kid? You're a disgrace to me and your entire family. I don't ever want to have anything to do with you again!"

Of course he wouldn't. Yet some people think of God as that kind of Father—one who rejects us when we stumble as we take our first hesitant steps on the Christian walk. No wonder people with that concept of God turn against Him! When we truly know the kind of gracious Father He is, we will love Him with all our hearts and gladly follow where He leads. Isn't that why He is so anxious that we learn to know Him?

How Jesus Dealt With Skeptics and Materialists

During Jesus' last days in the temple prior to His crucifixion, the Pharisees and Sadducees seemed to be taking turns trying to trip Him up. When the Pharisees were silenced, the Sadducees approached Him with artful questions. "The Sadducees rejected the traditions of the Pharisees. They professed to believe the greater portion of the Scriptures, and to regard them as the rule of action; but practically they were skeptics and materialists.

"The Sadducees denied the existence of angels, the resurrection of the dead, and the doctrine of a future life, with its rewards and punishments. On all these points they differed with the Pharisees. Between the two parties the resurrection was especially a subject of controversy" (*The Desire of Ages*, 603).

The Sadducees believed that God was superior to humans but argued that an overruling providence would deprive humanity of free moral agency and degrade humanity to slavery. "They held that man was free to control his own life and to shape the events of the world; that his destiny was in his own hands. They denied that the Spirit of God works through human efforts or natural means. Yet they still held that, through the proper employment of his natural powers, man could become elevated and enlightened; that by rigorous and austere exactions his life could be purified.

"Their ideas of God molded their own character. As in their view He had no interest in man, so they had little regard for one another; . . . Refusing to acknowledge the influence of the Holy Spirit upon human action, they lacked His power in their lives" (ibid., 604).

Christ's words and His works testified to a divine power that produces supernatural results and to a Father of the children who was ever watchful of their true interests. "He revealed the working of divine power in benevolence and compassion that rebuked the selfish exclusiveness of the Sadducees. . . . He showed the error of trusting to human power for that transformation of character which can be wrought only by the Spirit of God" (ibid., 605).

Feeling confident that they could bring Jesus into disrepute, the Sadducees chose to question Him on the resurrection. Their failure is outlined in Matthew 22:23-33. "Ye do err," He responded, "not knowing the Scriptures, nor the power of God (Matt. 22:29).

"The Sadducees had flattered themselves that they of all men adhered most strictly to the Scriptures. But Jesus showed that they had not known their true meaning. That knowledge must be brought home to the heart by the enlightenment of the Holy Spirit. Their ignorance of the Scriptures and the power of God He declared to be the cause of their confusion of faith and darkness of mind. They were seeking to bring the mysteries of God within the compass of their finite reasoning. . . . Thousands become infidels because their finite minds cannot comprehend the mysteries of God. They cannot explain the wonderful exhibition of divine power in His providences, therefore they reject the evidences of such power, attributing them to natural agencies which they can comprehend still less. The only key to the mysteries that surround us is to acknowledge in them all the presence and power of God. Men need to recognize God as the Creator of the universe, One who commands and executes all things. They need a broader view of His character, and of the mystery of His agencies" (ibid., 605, 606).

Chapter 3

GOD'S TWO WORDS

When I first met Ed Zinke, I recognized that he was a true intellectual. He believed that his was the right to pursue truth wherever it might lead and that reason was the means by which his knowledge of truth was to be tested. He describes his evolution from humanism to full acceptance of the authority of the Bible as follows: My education "taught me to question everything in the pursuit of truth. Everything, that is, except reason itself. Reason was sacrosanct; it was the unquestioned starting point for true knowledge; it was the Hubble through which humankind could view the universe without the distortion of superstition or the bondage of earthbound tunnel vision. . . .

"In my pursuit of a rational theology, I learned to apply the historical-critical method of study—basically, a humanistic approach to literature—to the Bible. My rationalistic and empirical presuppositions prepared me to accept the validity of this tool. Further, the method could be used to defend the Bible against the attacks of critics. The end surely justified the means. . . .

"If a theological concept seemed unworthy of my concept, I sought to reinterpret it. Fortunately, my concept of a God of love turned out to be pretty close to Bible truth, though I did not yet perceive that I was fitting God into my concept and judging Him by it; rather than fitting my concept into His Revelation. . . .

"I was tempted to think that . . . the biblical God of judgment had to be reinterpreted. The eradication of sinners could not be God's act. Rather, the sinner's fate was simply the result of his separating himself from the Lifegiver. Christ, by His death, did not take our sins upon Himself. Such a concept was foreign to rationality. What justice is there in one man dying in the place of another? The notion of a substutionary atonement was pagan. The cross, rationally interpreted, was only a manifestation of the love of God—there so powerfully expounded that the universe might be won over by this expression of divine concern. . . .

"But how was I to relate this God of my conception to the authority of Scripture, a notion somewhat confusing to me because it too was spoken in the context of rationality. . . .

"Such was my thinking as I began doctoral studies at the Catholic University of America. One of my early projects was to do a paper on the history of method in theology. Among other themes, the paper required argumentation for the authority of Scripture from a rational perspective.

"To my surprise, neither my professor nor my classmates bought my attempt to superimpose the authority of Scripture on my reasonable surmising. They argued that subjectivity precluded basing theology on the authority of Scripture. . . .

"How could I accept this if indeed my mind was the foundation and measure of truth? Had I not built a rock-solid foundation for faith on rationality? The idea of giving up the supremacy of my reason was frightening. . . .

"The conviction seized my soul: I was a humanist. I had elevated mind over God's Word, indeed, even over the One who sat on the throne of the universe. . . .

"Christ had declared Himself to be the Way, the Truth,

and the Life (John 14:6). But I had been trying to find truth apart from Him, so that I could do Him the favor of pulling Him into the canon of truth. I had attempted to make reason and sense data the standpoints from which truth could be seen, measured, and quantified. Now I saw that God intended His Word to play that role. . . .

"Furthermore, I saw that the Bible could not be interpreted from any other perspective or philosophical system, no matter how ancient or how modern. . . . The question was not which brand of humanism represented reality. Rather, it was a question of humanism versus the Word of God.

"*Sola Scriptura* also meant that the Bible must not be interpreted from the standpoint of any external methods. . . . [It should not] be subjected to the . . . historical-critical method. To do so would be to impose an alien culture upon the Word. The Bible was to be its own interpreter. Under the Holy Spirit the Word of God provides its own foundation, philosophical context, method of interpretation and general historical context. . . .

"The dividing line between the biblically based and the non-biblically based theologian is not doctrine but their respective attitudes toward the authority of the Bible. . . .

"As I negotiate uncharted pathways in my pilgrimage toward Truth, I rejoice in the power of God's Word. It brought worlds into existence. It gave sight to the blind, hearing to the deaf, life to the lifeless. When we read His Word, we're not confronting dead words on a page. It is as if God in person were speaking to us, and through the Holy Spirit seeking not only our heart but also our mind, our intellect. I now see His Word as self-authenticating, all sufficient, and able to instruct sinners, as He did me, in the way of salvation" (Edward Zinke, "Pilgrimage of a Believer," *Perspective Digest,* vol. 1, no. 3, 29-36).

The Bible does not attempt to prove that it is the Word of God. It claims divine authorship. The proof of this claim lies in what it is able to do for those who accept its claim. The Bible's origin as the Word of God gives it the living, unchanging, and demanding authority of God Himself.

Seventh-day Adventists believe in the two-sided, divine-human nature of revelation. "The Bible, with its God-given truths expressed in the language of men, presents a union of the divine and the human. Such a union existed in the nature of Christ, who was the Son of God and the Son of man. Thus it is true of the Bible, as it was of Christ, that 'the Word was made flesh, and dwelt among us.' John 1:14."—*The Great Controversy*, vi.

"It seems in harmony with the revealed truth of God to suggest that a similarity in principle prevails between the manner of the birth of the incarnate Word of God and the method of the composition of the written Word of God. Scripture was, so to speak, 'conceived or inspired of the Holy Ghost, and thought and uttered by human prophets.' Scripture is obviously the work of human writers; and yet it is still more the product and result of a special and supernormal activity of the Spirit" (Alan N. Stibbs, *Revelation and the Bible*, ed. C. F. H. Henry [Grand Rapids, Mich.: Baker Book House, 1949], 111).

The word *Bible* comes from the Greek word meaning "library." It is a collection of many ancient books, its first books having been written about 1500 B.C. and its last book about A.D. 100. There are thirty-nine books in the first section, which is known as the Old Testament, and twenty-seven books in the New Testament, making a total of sixty-six books in this collection. The Bible is unique, however, in that the men who wrote it did not merely write their own ideas. They "spake as they were moved by the Holy Ghost" (2 Pet. 1:21). About forty different writers served as God's penmen in the production of the Bible. These individuals lived and wrote in such widely scattered localities as Sinai, Babylon, Jerusalem, and Rome. God inspired various classes of writers. He used princes and paupers, heroes and herdsmen.

The Holy Spirit is able to preserve the divine within the human. In the same way that the divine and human natures were united in Jesus, divine thoughts were kept preserved by the Spirit within human expressions. Thus the Bible is at once fully human but more than human. Through its human words, thoughts, patterns, ideas, concepts, and history, God speaks.

Evidences That the Bible Is Inspired

The Bible's impressive harmony, in spite of its great diversity in authorship, time, and places written, is one of the unmistakable evidences that it is what it claims to be—the Word of God.

"The apostle Peter says that there are in Scripture 'things hard to be understood, which they that are unlearned and unstable wrest . . . unto their own destruction.' 2 Peter 3:16. The difficulties of Scripture have been urged by skeptics as an argument against the Bible; but so far from this, they constitute a strong evidence of its divine inspiration. . . . The very grandeur and mystery of the themes presented should inspire faith in it as the word of God.

"The Bible unfolds truth with a simplicity and a perfect adaptation to the needs and longings of the human heart, that has astonished and charmed the most highly cultivated minds, while it enables the humblest and uncultured to discern the way of salvation. . . . Thus the plan of redemption is laid open to us, so that every soul may see the steps he is to take in repentance toward God and faith toward our Lord Jesus Christ, in order to be saved in God's appointed way; yet beneath these truths, so easily understood, lie mysteries that are the hiding of His glory—mysteries that overpower the mind in its research, yet inspire the sincere seeker for truth with reverence and faith. The more he searches the Bible, the deeper is his conviction that it is the word of the living God, and human reason bows before the majesty of divine revelation" (*Steps to Christ*, 107, 108).

Among Bible writers there is an absolute certainty about the inspired nature of what other Bible writers have stated. You do not find Bible writers challenging the authenticity of what another has written.

Because God changes not, the revelation of His character in the Scriptures is unchanging. Because His way of saving lost men and women is one, the portrayal of that way in the Scriptures never can be changed or superseded. Because they are the word of God, they summon each of us to salvation and obedience. In a world of flux and change, of shifting values and conflicting claims of truth, they remain the one unerring standard.

The Key to Understanding the Bible

"They that seek the Lord understand all things." But it is not human reason or understanding that makes this possible. "Never should the Bible be studied without prayer. Before opening its pages we should ask for the enlightenment of the Holy Spirit, and it will be given" (*Steps to Christ,* 91). As we do so, we should lay aside all preconceived opinions and allow the Holy Spirit to guide us into truth. (See John 16:13.)

Why is the guidance of the Holy Spirit so essential in Bible study? As we approach the study of the Scriptures, we must remember their unique character. Ordinary means of investigation are inadequate. Many have seen the three-dimensional motion pictures that require special glasses to bring each scene into focus. God provides special glasses for us through the guidance of the Holy Spirit. The Spirit of truth in a special way focuses our attention on the plan of salvation.

Although we must compare scripture with scripture,

we must seek to understand fully what a passage says before we move on to other passages. We should not take it out of context, making the passage say something that God never intended it to say. One of the best ways of doing this is to "take one verse, and concentrate the mind on the task of ascertaining the thought which God has put in that verse for us. We should dwell upon the thought until it becomes our own, and we know 'what saith the Lord' " (*The Desire of Ages*, 390).

As we become better acquainted with God's will, what can we expect to happen in our lives? If the study of the Bible does not change our lives, we can be certain there is some fault in us. We cannot blame God. If we expect God to continue to guide us into additional revelations of His will, we must accept and put into practice the light He already has given us. (See John 7:17.)

"Every day you should learn something new from the Scriptures. Search them as for hid treasures, for they contain the words of eternal life. Pray for wisdom and understanding to comprehend these holy writings" (*My Life Today*, 22).

Those who "hear" and "do" that which Christ teaches are like the man who built his home on the solid rock (Luke 6:46-49). The floods mentioned in these verses represent the tests and trials of life. Faith that stands life's tests is built on careful and prayerful study of the Word of God.

The Word Reveals the Word

Wrongly viewed, even a Bible doctrine (for example, the destruction of the wicked) can present a false picture of what God is like. But studied with prayer and humility and with the Holy Spirit's immediate guidance, each Bible teaching becomes a picture that helps us see God more clearly. In a special way the Bible reveals God to us in Christ. Christ in turn is the clearest revelation of God's character that the world has ever seen. He is God's thought made audible. He is God's character made tangible. He is God's mind made understandable.

Christ suggests that as we "diligently study," we will find that "these are the Scriptures that testify about me" (John 5:39, NIV). We find Him to be the core, content, and context of these writings. If we take Jesus and His salvation out of the Bible, nothing substantial is left. All focuses on Him as the central good news. All Scripture is given by divine inspiration and is able to make us wise unto salvation through faith in Him (2 Tim. 3:15, 16).

In coming to the Bible, we discover that the Holy Spirit's mission is to lead us to Jesus, to glorify Him, and not the Holy Spirit Himself (John 16:13, 14). Because biblical writers wrote under inspiration of the Holy Spirit (2 Pet. 1:21), their focus also is on Jesus. Yet, to one unenlightened, or not guided by the Spirit, the Bible remains closed. To experience the purpose of the Scriptures, we must allow the Holy Spirit to lead us to encounter Christ therein and be led to glorify Him.

The subject of inspiration and revelation has become the key issue that divides the Adventist Church. Seventh-day Adventists reject the concept of a double source of revelation—the Bible plus tradition or experience or reason. We Adventists accept the Bible alone as the rule of our faith and practice. Any philosophical or scientific concept that disagrees with the clear teaching of God's Word cannot logically be included or accommodated in our theology.

How Jesus Dealt With the Question of Authority

"All the while Jesus was at Jerusalem during the feast [of Tabernacles] He was shadowed by spies. Day after day new schemes to silence Him were tried. The priests and rulers were watching to entrap Him. They were planning to stop Him by violence. But this was not all. They wanted to humble this Galilean rabbi before the people.

"On the first day of His presence at the feast, the rulers had come to Him, demanding by what authority He taught. They wished to divert attention from Him to the question of His right to teach, and thus to their own importance and authority.

"'My teaching is not Mine,' said Jesus, 'but His that sent Me. If any man willeth to do His will, he shall know of the teaching, whether it be of God, or whether I speak from Myself." John 7:16, 17, R. V. The question of these cavilers Jesus met, not by answering the cavil, but by opening up truth vital to the salvation of the soul. The perception and appreciation of truth, He said, depends less upon the mind than upon the heart. Truth must be received into the soul; it claims the homage of the will. If truth could be submitted to the reason alone, pride would be no hindrance in the way of its reception. But it is to be received through the work of grace in the heart; and its reception depends upon the renunciation of every sin that the Spirit of God reveals. Humanity's advantages for obtaining a knowledge of the truth, however great these may be, will prove of no benefit to them unless the heart is open to receive the truth and there is a conscientious surrender of every habit and practice that is opposed to its principles. To those who thus yield themselves to God, having an honest desire to know and to do His will, the truth is revealed as the power of God for their salvation. These will be able to distinguish between those who speak for God and those who speak merely from themselves. The Pharisees had not put their will on the side of God's will. They were not seeking to know the truth but to find some excuse for evading it; Christ showed that this was why they did not understand His teaching.

"He now gave a test by which the true teacher might be distinguished from the deceiver: 'He that speaketh from himself seeketh his own glory: but he that seeketh the glory of Him that sent him, the same is true, and no unrighteousness is in him.' John 7:18, R. V. He that seeketh his own glory is speaking only from himself. The spirit of self-seeking betrays its origin. But Christ was seeking the glory of God. He spoke the words of God. This was the evidence of His authority as a teacher of the truth" (*The Desire of Ages*, 455, 456).

Chapter 4

GOD DOESN'T REMOVE ALL ROOM FOR DOUBT

The words of the Bible have been transmitted to us in such a way that they bring us a trustworthy knowledge of God's plan of salvation and His instruction on how to live in order to get the most out of life. However, those who do not wish to follow God's instruction are prone to come up with lists of difficulties designed to demonstrate that the Bible cannot be the Word of God because it contradicts itself.

Ellen White describes how this takes place: "Those who think to make the supposed difficulties of Scripture plain, in measuring by their finite rule that which is inspired and that which is not inspired, had better cover their faces, as Elijah when the still small voice spoke to him; for they are in the presence of God and holy angels, who for ages have communicated to men light and knowledge, telling them what to do and what not to do, unfolding before them scenes of thrilling interest, waymark by waymark in symbols and signs and illustrations.

"And He [God] has not, while presenting the perils clustering about the last days, qualified any finite man to unravel hidden mysteries or inspired one man or any class of men to pronounce judgment as to that which is inspired or is not. When men, in their finite judgment, find it necessary to go into an examination of scriptures to define that which is inspired and that which is not, they have stepped before Jesus to show Him a better way than He has led us. . . .

"Human minds vary. The minds of different education and thought receive different impressions of the same words, and it is difficult for one mind to give to one of a different temperament, education, and habits of thought by language exactly the same idea as that which is clear and distinct in his own mind. Yet to honest men, right-minded men, he can be so simple and plain as to convey his meaning for all practical purposes. If the man he communicates with is not honest and will not want to see and understand the truth, he will turn his words and language in everything to suit his own purposes. He will misconstrue his words, play upon his imagination, wrest them from their true meaning, and then entrench himself in unbelief, claiming that the sentiments are all wrong" (*Selected Messages*, 1:17, 19).

During one summer when I was attending Pacific Union College, I worked as a bellboy in the Fairmont Hotel in San Francisco. One of the older bellboys didn't like the idea that I was studying for the ministry. Several times during that summer he confronted me with a question he considered to be able to stump anyone who believed in the Bible. His question was "Who married Cain?" My reply was "He married one of his sisters. See Genesis 5:4." But a few weeks later he'd corner me and ask that question again, apparently not remembering the last time I had answered it. Because it was his classic excuse for not believing the Bible, he didn't pay any attention to the way the Bible answered his question.

One of the "happy hunting grounds" for those who make much of the so-called difficulties in the Bible is the apparent discrepancy as to the words used in the inscription on the cross.

Matt. 27:37—THIS IS JESUS THE KING OF THE JEWS

Mark 15:26—THE KING OF THE JEWS

Luke 23:38—THIS IS THE KING OF THE JEWS

John 19:19—JESUS OF NAZARETH THE KING OF THE JEWS

John, standing at the foot of the cross for those long dreadful hours had the most opportunity to study the inscription. The usual form of such an inscription included the condemned man's name, place of residence, and the offense as we find outlined in John 19:19. The other Gospel writers give a summary of the titles on the cross. Many see one of John's purposes in writing his Gospel as adding details missing in the three Synoptic Gospels. Thus, you would expect him to play this role in the case of the inscription. The indictment also was written in three languages: Hebrew (Aramaic), Greek, and Latin. This provides another reason why some translations may be incomplete. Instead of recording the differences in translation from three inscriptions, some writers may have just been summarizing the intent. The main point is that all four testify to an inscription that mentions Jesus being crucified for claiming He was the king of the Jews. Most readers are not bothered by these kinds of differences, but some from the historicocritical school make mountains out of molehills.

The best answer to the critics is to understand the process by which God revealed His written Word. When we do, we'll approach our Bible study from positive assumptions rather than negative ones. Peter states clearly that "holy men of God spake as they were moved by the Holy Ghost" (2 Pet. 1:21). Although the Scriptures were not written until the time of Moses and later, before that time the patriarchs and prophets presented God's messages in oral form. God spoke to Noah, and Noah spoke to the world for God. When Jacob blessed Joseph's sons, he laid his right hand upon the head of Ephraim. Joseph objected, explaining that because Manasseh was the firstborn, Jacob's right hand should be placed on him. But Jacob refused, stating under inspiration that Manasseh's "younger brother shall be greater than he" (Gen. 48:19).

The Holy Spirit "moved" upon the prophets to enable them to present accurately to others the messages God gave them to deliver. This does not mean that the Holy Spirit dictated the words. The prophets were God's pen-men, not His pen. But the Holy Spirit worked carefully with each writer preventing the inclusion of falsehoods. What many of the critics deny is that God is able to so work with the free creativity and literary expressions of those to whom he has given the gift of prophecy that they become his spokespersons for the truth. He did just that. The Bible we have today is the inspired Word of God and the infallible revelation of His will and "the standard of character, the revealer of doctrines, and the test of experience" (*The Great Controversy*, vii).

Two passages make it clear that God cannot lie. Hebrews 6:18 states that it is "impossible for God to lie." John 17:17 adds that God's "word is truth." Therefore God by nature cannot use intentional falsehoods in order to bolster the presentation of truth. Bible writers did not accommodate what they had to say to the mistaken views of their day. Because God *is* truth He never does lie.

An erroneous Bible has no authority but is subject to whatever human opinions are interpreting it. Inspiration guarantees that we can accept everything affirmed in the Scriptures as God-given truth. The prophets used their own languages in a way that was familiar to them and a literary style that is ordinarily quite distinct from that which characterized the other prophets but were guided in their understanding in such a way that we can have confidence that the thoughts they expressed were God's thoughts.

So-called Bible "Mistakes"

Many of the discrepancies critics through the ages have pointed out as making it difficult to accept the Bible as the infallible revelation of God involve minor differences in arithmetic, descriptions, or small details. To most Bible students who accept the Bible fully as God-inspired, such issues are not important. But they do become significant stumbling blocks to those who use these so-called "mistakes" to demonstrate what they consider to be the unreliability of the Bible. Doing so makes the human mind the final arbiter of truth. Satan can use the critics to raise more and more questions than Bible scholars have time to answer. Apparently he is trying to sidetrack us from the positive work of sharing God's truth by getting us to spend a lot of unnecessary effort in meeting objections. But if we are patient we'll find that after a while other critics will come along who contradict the positions taken by earlier critics. The samples of criticisms below only touch on what many see as discrepancies.

Araunah or Ornan—2 Samuel 24 or 1 Chronicles 21. Whose threshing floor did David purchase? Was it Ornan's or was it Araunah's? People who see a conflict here do not understand the variations implicit in spelling Semitic names. They both were called Jebusites who owned a threshing floor near Jerusalem. The accounts identify them as the same person. Why then the difference in names? Did one writer make a mistake? The *SDA Bible Dictionary* identifies them as the same person: "*Araunah or Ornan.* [Heb. '*Arawanah,* '*Awarna,* '*Aranyah, and* '*Ornan*]. The name has not yet been fully explained, but it is almost certain that it is related to Hurrian" (pp. 70,

71). What is clear is that these are merely variants of the same name.

One or two?—How many angels appeared at Christ's tomb—one (Matt. 28:5) or two (John 20:12)? How many demoniacs did Jesus heal at Gadara—one (Luke 8:27) or two (Matt. 8:28)? The answer is two. There are many reasons why a Bible writer might put emphasis on one person or angel being reported without mentioning another. In neither of these cases does the text indicate that there was *only one.* Obviously where there are two there has to be at least one, but if it is two you must have more than one.

Date of Daniel—Porphyry (A.D. 233–304) placed the writing of Daniel in the second century B.C. in order to reduce the impact of fulfilled prophecies. In recent years there was a smattering of some following his example in the Adventist Church. But such an explanation does not account for the 490-year prophecy of Daniel 9 that points to the ministry and death of Jesus 300 years later, not to say anything about the 1260- and 2300-year prophecies.

Portrayal of Christ's Words on the Cross in Psalm 22— Anyone who has read the Gospels cannot help noticing that Psalm 22 foretells some of Jesus' sayings on the cross. The psalm is talking about David's personal experience with suffering. Critics believe that the New Testament writers who quote Psalm 22 as being fulfilled at the cross are reinterpreting the psalm to fit their own perspective. But David's experience does not encompass all the trauma nor match all the incidents implied in the psalm. This is one key to understanding that the Holy Spirit had a prophetic fulfillment in mind when inspiring David to pen these words. Another key is that it was the same Spirit who influenced the New Testament writers to apply the experience of Psalm 22 to Jesus on the cross. Whenever an inspired writer applies a text in a different way, he is not reinterpreting but helping us find deeper meaning in a later application of a type or prophecy.

Room for Doubt

The reliability of Scripture has been confirmed on every hand from such disparate fields as archeology, geology, and many other "ologies" that give us clear evidence that the Bible is accurate in its portrayal of that which took place long ago. Biblical truths such as Creation taking place in six literal days, the universal flood, and Jesus raising the dead cannot be rightly subjected to "scientific" opinion. Yet each of these have been. This not only tells us something about the extent of human pride and intellectual arrogance but also indicates that God has seen that it is best not to remove the possibility of doubt.

"God never asks us to believe, without giving sufficient evidence upon which to base our faith. His existence, His character, the truthfulness of His word, are all established by testimony that appeals to our reason; and this testimony is abundant. Yet God has never removed the possibility of doubt" (*Steps to Christ,* 105). "The word of God, like the character of its Author, presents mysteries that can never be fully comprehended by finite beings. . . . True, He has not removed the possibility of doubt; faith must rest upon evidence, not demonstration; those who wish to doubt have opportunity; but those who desire to know the truth find ample ground for faith" (*Education*, 169).

It sounds as if we must choose on which wall of the "belief/doubt" entryway we hang our cloak of faith. When that is settled, we can build on our choice—whether it be a positive direction to a growing faith or a decision to doubt. How do we grow faith? One answer seen recently on a church bulletin board carries a most thoughtful message: "Feed your faith, and your doubt will starve to death."

Have you ever seen a miracle? Would you like to? Pick

up your Bible and look at it. It's a real miracle—in the way it was produced and transmitted and in the way the Spirit uses it to move upon your heart and life. At this point in the history of sin and salvation we are in desperate need of both kinds of miracles in our personal lives and in our church.

How Jesus Dealt With Doubt, Unbelief, and Rejection

"In every age there is given to men their day of light and privilege, a probationary time in which they may become reconciled to God. But there is a limit to this grace. Mercy may plead for years and be slighted and rejected; but there comes a time when mercy makes her last plea. The heart becomes so hardened that it ceases to respond to the Spirit of God. Then the sweet, winning voice entreats the sinner no longer, and reproofs and warnings cease.

"That day had come to Jerusalem. Jesus wept in anguish over the doomed city, but He could not deliver her. He had exhausted every resource. In rejecting the warnings of God's Spirit, Israel had rejected the only means of help. There was no other power by which they could be delivered.

"The Jewish nation was a symbol of the people of all ages who scorn the pleadings of Infinite Love. The tears of Christ when He wept over Jerusalem were for the sins of all time. In the judgments pronounced upon Israel, those who reject the reproofs and warnings of God's Holy Spirit, may read their own condemnation.

"In this generation there are many who are treading on the same ground as were the unbelieving Jews. They have witnessed the manifestation of the power of God; the Holy Spirit has spoken to their hearts; but they cling to their unbelief and resistance. God sends them warnings and reproof, but they are not willing to confess their errors, and they reject His message and His messenger. The very means He uses for their recovery becomes to them a stone of stumbling.

"The prophets of God were hated by apostate Israel because through them their hidden sins were brought to light. Ahab regarded Elijah as his enemy because the prophet was faithful to rebuke the king's secret iniquities. So today the servant of Christ, the reprover of sin, meets with scorn and rebuffs. Bible truth, the religion of Christ, struggles against a strong current of moral impurity. Prejudice is even stronger in the hearts of men now than in Christ's day. Christ did not fulfill men's expectations; His life was a rebuke to their sins, and they rejected Him. So now the truth of God's word does not harmonize with men's practices and their natural inclination, and thousands reject its light. Men prompted by Satan cast doubt upon God's word, and choose to exercise their independent judgment. They choose darkness rather than light, but they do it at the peril of their souls. Those who caviled at the words of Christ found ever-increased cause for cavil, until they turned from the Truth and the Life. So it is now. God does not propose to remove every objection which the carnal heart may bring against His truth. To those who refuse the precious rays of light which would illuminate the darkness, the mysteries of God's word remain such forever. From them the truth is hidden. They walk blindly, and know not the ruin before them" (*The Desire of Ages,* 587, 588).

Chapter 5

THE UNIQUENESS OF THE GIFT OF PROPHECY

I call Amos the nonprophet prophet. Why? Amos climaxed his response to his critics with the statement "I am not a prophet" (Amos 7:14). Basically, he was saying: "I'm not a professional prophet. I'm chosen by God to be His messenger to you. Don't blame me for telling you what God told me to tell you!" As did Ellen White nearly two millennia later, Amos was saying "I'm merely a humble person God chose to be His messenger. Other than that, I make no claims."

It was a time of peace, prosperity, and pleasure-seeking. A time when there had been an unprecedented increase in the number of wealthy people who lived in luxury and indulgence. Their extravagance contrasted with the misery of the poor. Cities were growing rapidly at the expense of rural development. The judges were dishonest, the government corrupt. Justice had become a joke. Extortion, crime, and class hatred were visible on every hand. Wealthy women were pampered, wearing expensive clothing and cosmetics. Overuse of alcoholic beverages contributed to crime and indecency. Immorality was rampant, and incest was common. Robbery and murder had increased tremendously. Terrible, devastating disasters plagued the land. Most people claimed to be religious but lived lives that denied a true experience with God. Although a variety of religious forms attracted people, the major religion was self-worship. There had been terrible signs of impending military destruction, but the threats had passed. Sounds like America as it approaches the third millennium, doesn't it? But it was Israel in the 700s B.C.

Who did God call to attempt to put a halt to this self-indulgent way of life? He chose one of the humblest of the humble. He was a shepherd at a time when shepherds were looked down upon and a "dresser of sycamore fruit." He lived on the edge of the desert where the inhabitants didn't have access to the milk and honey of the land just to the north. The so-called sycamore fig was used by the poorer people to sustain life. To "dress" it, Amos had to climb a tree with a knife in hand to slit each "fig" to let a bitter juice run out. It also is thought that the opening would allow insects to get into the fruit. There they would lay their maggots that would ferment the fruit, making it more edible.

This rough man of the desert had no problem describing the faults of the people in clear but earthy language. For instance in chapter 4:1, he refers to the pampered women who had been pushing their husbands to provide more luxuries for them as the "cows of Bashan." Interestingly, this rough man was used by the Holy Spirit to present an attack on the sins of Israel in the most tactful way possible. Even though eventually he was ordered out of Israel by its wicked king and sent back to the land of Judah from which he began his missionary tour, he attracted large crowds to hear his message of fiery judgment to come if the people did not repent.

The conditions of Amos's day were comparable to ours; the messages of judgment and impending natural disasters serve as a warning to this last wicked generation and apply equally with the warnings given by Ellen White to our age. Amos 3:7 states: "Surely the Lord God will do nothing, but he revealeth his secret unto his servants the prophets." The context is that of warning about judgments. The prophets came in major blocs prior to the crises God's people faced. A block of eighth-century prophets gave warning of the Assyrian conquest of Israel. Another block of seventh-century prophets warned of the Babylonian captivity. Another group was sent to shepherd the people through the captivity and another to minister during the crisis of the return from exile and the rebuilding of Jerusalem and the temple. Certainly, God would be expected to send a prophet to help prepare the world for its great final crisis just before the return of Christ. It would be difficult to believe that we are living in the end-time crisis if God had not sent us His messenger.

Many current theologians think that they have to establish their credentials by "learned" critiques of God's messengers and messages. But rather than establishing their credentials as proclaimers of the truths of God, their criticisms expose them as false prophets. Those who claim to have "new light" that contradicts "old light" merely demonstrate that they have "no light" (see Isa. 8:20). One thing is clear about the last-day manifestation of the gift of prophecy. Christ's warning against false prophets in the last days establishes clearly that there will be a manifestation of the true gift. If there were only false prophets, He would have warned against anyone claiming to manifest the gift in the last-day church.

Three Bible passages indicate strongly that there will be a last-day prophetic gift.

Joel 2:28-32 was partially fulfilled at Pentecost (see Acts 2:16-21), but the greatest fulfillment takes place in the last days when the signs mentioned in verses 30, 31 also take place. Ephesians 4:11-14 seems to suggest that there is one major reason why the spirit of prophecy is needed in the last days. Verse 12 literally states: "With a view to the mending of the saints for the purpose of the work of Christ unto the house building of the body of Christ." The gift will be needed until we come into "the unity of the faith . . . unto the measure of the stature of the fulness of Christ" (verse 13). Revelation 12:17 and 19:10 specifies that the remnant church of the last days will have "the testimony of Jesus," which is the "spirit of prophecy."

The Last-Day Gift of Prophecy

Selection of the prophet is the only church appointment that God has kept strictly in His own hands. Prophecy comes not "by the will of man." Note these illustrations:

a. Prophets sometimes prophesied without foreseeing that they would (1 Kings 13:20-22).
b. Prophets sometimes prophesied when they did not want to and could not always do what they wanted to do (Num. 23:12, 20; 24:13).
c. Considering that so many careful Bible scholars today have to go back about two thousand years to find the prophetic gift in action, we Adventists are privileged to have the prophetic gift. It leads us to a better knowledge of how inspiration works.

Let me illustrate this special advantage by what happened to my great-grandfather.

"Listen, Joseph," said the bishop, "that man Bates is back here in southern Michigan stirring up people with his notions about Saturday being the Sabbath. Because you're one of our strongest preachers, I want you to lead out in driving Bates out of Michigan. Suppose you go everywhere he goes and meet his arguments. Will you do that?"

"Certainly, Bishop," Joseph chuckled. "That shouldn't

be so difficult. Everyone knows that the Saturday Sabbath was just for the children of Israel and that we're living under the new covenant. I don't anticipate much trouble in setting things straight."

Michigan was part of "the West" in those days. The southern part was not heavily forested but was dotted with small prairies and clearings. Jackson was a town of about three thousand people, and it was here that Captain Bates had raised up the first group of Adventists in Michigan. In June and July 1852 he made another visit to this busy little town.

That summer "the war was on" between the two Josephs—Bates and Frisbie—and it wasn't long before the popular Methodist preacher saw that it was not going to be easy to answer Bates's arguments.

Joseph Frisbie had always been a careful Bible student and a man of conviction. Several years before this, he had been led to the study of the question of nonimmortality of the soul through the writings of George Storrs. He had accepted the Bible teaching without hesitation, although it was contrary to the doctrine of his denomination. Later study also convinced him that baptism should be performed by immersion. However, he was certain that the Saturday Sabbath had only been given to the children of Israel, and he was bitterly opposed to its teaching.

Joseph Frisbie had married Delpha Jane Glover in Sylvan, Michigan, in June 1847. One of Delpha Jane's brothers, Lorin, built his home at Sylvan, which was about twelve miles east of Jackson and had a fine, large barn there, conveniently situated for a gathering place.

When Captain Bates visited Lorin one day to ask for the use of the barn for his meetings, Lorin laughed and said, "I guess so. My sister's husband is a preacher, and he's been saying some pretty hard things about you. We'll have him come over too, and we'll see who's right."

On a moonlit July night the people from the surrounding farms walked down the winding lanes to Lorin Glover's barn. Rough-hewn planks were laid out on boxes for seats. A crude platform had been hastily set up at the far end of the building where a string of lanterns lighted up the strange charts that Captain Bates was arranging on the wall.

The crowd was excited at the prospect of a debate. Elder Frisbie, whose home was in nearby Chelsea, was well-liked by these people. He was a tall man and rather handsome with his dark hair, straight nose, flashing blue eyes, and curly black beard. They respected him as a Bible scholar and a man of principle.

The audience riveted their attention on Bates as he pointed to the charts and began to explain the prophecies. When he had finished, Frisbie announced, "I can't disagree with anything that has been presented tonight. It was all right from the Bible. But I imagine that after tomorrow night's lecture I'll have something to say!"

Not until two nights later did Bates introduce the Sabbath question. Frisbie, who was the more practiced speaker of the two, swayed the audience with the power of his reply. Captain Bates quietly answered him with scriptures that clearly disproved Joseph's thesis that the law was not binding on Christians under the new covenant.

That night, after the family was in bed, Joseph sat up searching his Bible to find the truth about the Sabbath. Whenever, in the course of that night, he was confronted with a difficulty that seemed more than his own mind could solve, he would drop to his knees and pray the problem through. By early morning he was overwhelmingly convinced that Bates was right.

The evening following his all-night study session, a determined Joseph Frisbie faced the growing crowd in Lorin's barn. Almost fiercely he told how he had spent the night before, searching the Scriptures. "But nowhere," he admitted, "have I been able to find one text that refutes the teachings of Captain Bates."

After the surprise of this sudden announcement, Joseph Bates lectured to a hushed audience that listened with new respect and attention.

The last lecture of the series in the barn at Sylvan Center was unforgettable. Captain Bates called for those to stand who had become convinced that the Bible teaching of the seventh-day Sabbath was right and intended to keep it. The audience stirred uneasily. Finally Lorin Glover stood to his feet. His wife and family joined him. Over on the other side of the barn, father William Glover rose quietly. Next to Joseph there was a rustling of skirts. People looked around, hardly believing what they saw. Delpha Jane Frisbie, hesitantly at first then with full determination, stood to her feet. Her husband remained rigidly in his seat.

On their way home after the meeting Joseph finally broke the silence. "Delpha Jane, you do what you think is right. I can't join you right now. I believe, too, that the seventh day is the Sabbath. But how can I give up my pastoral work that means more than my very life to me?

When the bishop visited Joseph again, his white beard, which extended nearly to his rather paunchy waist, began to tremble as Joseph told him that his personal study of the Bible had convinced him that Bates was right about the Sabbath.

The bishop pleaded. "Just forget these foolish notions and I'll see that you're given the largest city church in the state for your pastorate." This was a tempting offer. But as Joseph continued to search through the Bible, he became more and more convinced that if he were to please God, he must keep the seventh-day Sabbath. During the weeks that followed, he became fast friends with Joseph Bates. He even invited the old sea captain into his pulpits on Sunday mornings to teach the truth about the Sabbath and the second coming of Jesus.

But Frisbie could find no peace of mind until on March 1, 1853, he severed connections with his former denomination and began to devote his life to preaching the Sabbath and Advent messages. He was thirty-six years old when he gave up his minister's salary. Having had some experience at the mason's trade, he began searching for jobs of plastering, laying brick, carpenter work, or gardening. Whenever he had accumulated enough to take care of his family for a while, he would lay down his tools and put on his dark preacher's suit. Taking his horse and buggy, he would go off among his former friends and parishioners, teaching them the precious new truth until his money was gone.

"I've been invited to a meeting over in Jackson," Joseph told Delpha Jane one evening at supper. It was three months since he had begun keeping the Sabbath. "It's going to be at Dan Palmer's place. He's the blacksmith in Jackson and a firm believer in the three angels' messages."

In the Palmers' large two-story frame house, Joseph first met Elder J. N. Loughborough and James and Ellen White. Mrs. White was given a vision at this meeting in which she saw Joseph Frisbie. Afterward she told him that it was revealed to her that "God had arrested a soul by the light and power of the truth, and that through him He would get glory to Himself."

Elder White, reporting this meeting in the *Review and Herald*, wrote feelingly of their first contact as follows: "Brother J. B. Frisbie . . . spoke freely of his former prejudices and opposition to the Sabbath and Sabbath keepers, the change that had taken place in his feelings and views, and that he was now with us in sentiment and in sympathy. We first saw this dear brother at the Jackson Conference, and when introduced to him shook the friendly hand of him who had so strongly opposed us. . . . Our feelings could not be easily described. . . . We both wept, and there mingled our tears of gratitude and joy" (*Review and Herald,* 4:29).

A few weeks later Joseph was invited to attend a general meeting at the home of the Whites in Rochester, New York.

After the Rochester conference, Joseph spent August and September traveling through southern Michigan. It seemed good to him to counsel and visit with the few scattered Adventists along the way. He couldn't resist trying to convert some of his former minister friends. In his report to Elder White he wrote, "We had a very pleasant visit with our old friend, J. P. Weeks, who has formerly been a Union preacher. We laid the truth before him as well as we could and left him to investigate, praying the Lord to bless."

The old home in Chelsea wasn't the same now for the once-popular Joseph. It was as if the devil had thrown up a wall between the townspeople and their former minister. One day, a bit sadly, he said to his wife, "Let's take our horse and buggy and visit the places where I have preached, and ask God to help us find the location where He wants us to work for Him."

They drove to Grass Lake, to Jackson, then to Marshall and Ceresco. But they were not impressed to stay and work in any of these places. When they reached the bustling town of Battle Creek, which in the early 1850s boasted some two thousand inhabitants, Joseph said, "Dell, I feel impressed that this is the place where the Lord wants us to stay."

Going to the post office, he asked Mr. Noble, the postmaster, if he knew of anyone in town who observed the seventh day of the week for the Sabbath.

"There's a man out in the West End, name of Hewitt, who keeps Saturday for Sunday, just cross the bridge over the creek to Van Buren Street and go west. David Hewitt's house is on the right, just before Cass Street." Finding Brother Hewitt, who seemed overjoyed at this meeting with a fellow believer, Joseph announced, "God has impressed my family and me that we should locate here and help with the work in this place. Do you know where we can find a place to live?"

There weren't any houses for rent in that part of town. But there were two good lots on the corner of Cass and Van Buren streets that the preacher might be able to purchase for twenty-five dollars each. It didn't take Joseph long to make arrangements for the property. In a few days he set about building a board-and-batten house on the corner lots.

Joseph had taken an interest in a young man named Merritt Cornell before either had become a Sabbath keeper. He had Merritt open the meetings for him and encouraged him to preach. In 1854 Cornell had been sent to purchase the first tent to be used for evangelistic meetings. That same year Joseph and Merritt held several tent meetings together in Battle Creek and elsewhere. In 1855 Frisbie helped build the first Battle Creek church on his property at Cass and Van Buren streets.

Joseph served his Lord faithfully as a Seventh-day Adventist minister for twenty-nine years. Failing health in later years made it difficult for him to devote the same amount of energy to his work that he had during the pioneer days in Michigan. In the 1860s the Lord began sending messages through Ellen White warning against gathering in too large numbers at Battle Creek. Among the first to heed the instruction to go elsewhere was Joseph Frisbie. He moved his family back to the old home in

Chelsea, about sixty miles from Battle Creek. Here he labored faithfully until his death.

In the spring of 1882 he received a card from an old minister friend, O. R. L. Crosier. The message said:

"Dear Brother,
I am here at Brother Edward Fuller's. . . . I expect to be in Chelsea next week, Wednesday, March 1 . . . would like a religious visit.
(Signed) O. R. L. Crosier"

When Crosier arrived, the Frisbies invited him to stay overnight with the family. The next morning Joseph invited his guest into the parlor and talked with him for several hours about the Adventist faith. Soon the conversation turned to Mrs. White and the visions.

Joseph told Crosier the story of his first meeting with the Whites in Jackson where Mrs. White had seen him in vision and had informed him that it was God's purpose for him to become an Adventist minister.

At the conference of 1856 he had witnessed Mrs. White in vision again. On that occasion James White had invited all who wished to do so to examine the physical phenomena of her vision. Joseph had done so and had been awed by what he had seen.

Joseph also related to Crosier how at a later period he had been discouraged by poor health and had decided to give up the ministry in favor of farming in Kansas. Just before the move, Joseph attended a conference in Battle Creek. Mrs. White called him aside and told him that again she had seen him in vision. She was shown the trials and discouragements he had been through. She revealed certain things that no person other than Joseph himself could possibly have known about his experiences. Then she told him that it was not God's will for him to move to Kansas but that he should continue in the ministry.

Joseph was not "disobedient to the heavenly vision" but threw his whole heart and soul into the work again, encouraged by this definite message from heaven.

As Joseph concluded his testimony to Crosier, emphasizing how much the Spirit of prophecy had meant to him personally, he noted that his guest was pacing back and forth across the room. Finally Crosier sat down. He leaned forward in his chair and asked earnestly, "Elder Frisbie, do you really think there is anything in the visions?"

"There is no doubt whatsoever in my mind but that Mrs. White is the inspired prophet of God," Joseph answered, weighing every word thoughtfully.

Crosier, who had accepted the sanctuary truth and the Sabbath in the early days but eventually had turned bitterly against both, was greatly impressed by this testimony. It was one of Joseph Frisbie's last opportunities to witness to his belief in inspiration.

How Jesus Met Questions About the Prophetic Gift

"Like the stars in the vast circuit of their appointed path, God's purposes know no haste and no delay. Through the symbols of the great darkness and the smoking furnace, God had revealed to Abraham the bondage of Israel in Egypt, and had declared that the time of their sojourning should be four hundred years. 'Afterward,' He said, 'shall they come out with great substance.' Gen. 15:14. Against that word, all the power of Pharaoh's proud empire battled in vain. On 'the self-same day' appointed in the divine promise, 'it came to pass, that all the hosts of the Lord went out from the land of Egypt.' Exod. 12:41. So in heaven's council the hour for the coming of Christ had been determined. When the great clock of time pointed to that hour, Jesus was born in Bethlehem. . . .

"As the Jews had departed from God, faith had grown dim, and hope had well-nigh ceased to illuminate the future. The words of the prophets were uncomprehended. To the masses of the people, death was a dread mystery; beyond was uncertainty and gloom. It was not alone the wailing of the mothers of Bethlehem, but the cry from the great heart of humanity, that was borne to the prophet across the centuries,—the voice heard in Ramah, 'lamentation, and weeping, and great mourning, Rachel weeping for her children, and would not be comforted, because they are not.' Matt. 2:18. In 'the region and shadow of death,' men sat unsolaced. With longing eyes they looked for the coming of the Deliverer, when the darkness should be dispelled, and the mystery of the future should be made plain. . . .

"For hundreds of years the Scriptures had been translated into the Greek language, then widely spoken throughout the Roman Empire. The Jews were scattered everywhere, and their expectation of the Messiah's coming was to some extent shared by the Gentiles. Among those whom the Jews styled heathen were men who had a better understanding of the Scripture prophecies concerning the Messiah than had the teachers in Israel. There were some who hoped for His coming as a deliverer from sin. Philosophers endeavored to study into the mystery of the Hebrew economy. But the bigotry of the Jews hindered the spread of the light. Intent on maintaining the separation between themselves and other nations, they were unwilling to impart the knowledge they still possessed concerning the symbolic service. . . .

"Lessons must be given to humanity in the language of humanity. The Messenger of the covenant must speak. His voice must be heard in His own temple. Christ must come to utter words which should be clearly and definitely understood. He, the author of truth, must separate truth from the chaff of man's utterance, which had made it of no effect. The principles of God's government and the plan of redemption must be clearly defined. The lessons of the Old Testament must be fully set before men. Satan was exulting that he had succeeded in debasing the image of God in humanity. Then Jesus came to restore in man the image of his maker. None but Christ can fashion anew the character that has been ruined by sin. He came to expel the demons that had controlled the will. He came to lift us up from the dust, to reshape the marred character after the pattern of His divine character, and to make it beautiful with His own glory" (*The Desire of Ages,* 32-38).

Chapter 6

STONES CRYING OUT

Under the sponsorship of wealthy Lord Carnarvon, Howard Carter engaged in off and on archeological exploration in the area of the ancient Egyptian city of Thebes beginning in 1908. The two had been responsible for several interesting discoveries, but World War I nearly stopped their explorations. From 1919 to 1921, Carter worked over the entire section of the Valley of the Kings between the tombs of Merneptah, Ramses III, and Ramses IV. Still no important discovery was made, and the concession to dig there had only a few more weeks to run.

Carter had just about given up hope of making a major discovery in that area when, on the morning of November 4, 1922, he found a rough-hewn stair step below the entry to Ramses IV's tomb. Following this lead, he uncovered the entrance to another royal tomb—one that was to prove more fabulous in the richness of its contents than any other Egyptian royal sepulcher found up to that time. As he came to the barrier across the passageway, Carter was able to read the hieroglyphic inscription, which indicated that the occupant of the tomb was the long-sought Tutankhamen.

Excitedly, Carter summoned Lord Carnarvon from England. The wealthy patron and his daughter arrived in

Alexandria on November 20. On November 25, the first stone was removed from the tomb wall, allowing Carter, Lord Carnarvon, and Carnarvon's daughter, Lady Evelyn Herbert, to catch the first breathtaking glimpse of the strange golden animals, statues, and furniture that have now become world famous. The treasure they discovered that memorable day is said to be one of the greatest single discoveries of concentrated wealth. Because King Tut ruled in Egypt during the time of the judges in Israel, this discovery shed much light on the customs, practices, and philosophies of that era, thus helping us to understand the Bible better.

This is only one of the many discoveries in the last one hundred years or so that has contributed greatly to our understanding of Bible times.

How Was the Bible Produced?

"During the first twenty-five hundred years of human history, there was no written revelation. Those who had been taught of God, communicated their knowledge to others, and it was handed down from father to son, through successive generations. The preparation of the written word began in the time of Moses. Inspired revelations were then embodied in an inspired book. This work continued during the long period of sixteen hundred years—from Moses, the historian of creation and the law, to John, the recorder of the most sublime truths of the gospel" (*The Great Controversy*, v).

Not only did the Holy Spirit inspire the production of the Bible, but He also supernaturally preserved those Scriptures that He wanted people of later ages to have and to study. The Bible is a miracle book not only in its inception but also in its transmission to us. When we accept it as it is—the fully inspired Word of God—it becomes a very precious means of daily communication with God.

No matter how highly we regard the Bible, the Scriptures will be only of minimal use unless we let the Holy Spirit help us understand what God's will is for us and be willing to practice what God preaches.

Not all of the writings of the prophets were preserved for future generations. But the Bible, as we know it, was preserved in its present form for those of us who live in the end times.

Although many critics attack the form and structure of God's revelation, we must take into account that it was *God* who chose the form He saw was best for getting the Bible to us. He *will* be heard today—even if the very stones will have to cry out as He predicted they might to those religious leaders who were rejecting Him during His triumphal procession.

Burning with malice, the Pharisees who witnessed the scene did everything they could to silence the people; but their appeals and threats only increased the enthusiasm. The rulers pressed through the crowd and accosted Jesus, demanding, " 'Master, rebuke Thy disciples.' " In reply Jesus uttered these significant words: " 'I tell you that, if these should hold their peace, the stones would immediately cry out.' " That scene of triumph had been foretold by the prophet Zechariah. Humans were powerless to stop it. Had the people been bullied into failing to carry out God's will, a voice would have been given to the inanimate stones, and they would have hailed Christ as king. How blind those Pharisees were! The people praising Jesus recognized the event as being a fulfillment of Zechariah's prophecy, but the religious leaders were so blinded by their determination to reject Him that they seemingly paid no attention to the words of prophecy the crowd actually was singing.

In another sense the stones are crying out today. I don't believe it was an accident that after the humanistic and critical theories began to sweep through the theological world, the Lord inspired a new interest in biblical archeology. And it is fascinating how many of the discoveries add new light to and support for the Scriptures.

Amarna Tablets

Late in the nineteenth century an Egyptian woman, rummaging in the ruins of Amarna, discovered a large number of ancient letters in the Akkadian language, written on baked clay tablets. Stuffing them in gunnysacks, she sold them for a pittance to a local tradesman. The tradesman loaded the sacks on donkeys and gave them a rough 200-mile ride to Cairo. It was an unprofitable trip for him, however, as the Cairo antiquity dealers refused to buy them, being suspicious that they were forgeries, as no clay tablets written in cuneiform had ever been found in Egypt.

The sacks of tablets were reloaded on the donkeys and transported to Luxor, 400 miles south of Cairo. By the time a scholar in Luxor recognized their value, many of the tablets had been broken. They were soon purchased by museums and an astonished world learned that hundreds of these were letters, diplomatic correspondence, and dispatches from officials in western Asia to kings of the Egyptian Amarna Period. The Amarna letters, as they now are known, are dated about 1400–1360 B.C., which is the approximate time of the Israelite invasion of Canaan under Joshua. They shed valuable light on conditions in Palestine and Egypt at that time. These little gray tablets greatly enlarge the Bible student's understanding of events only hinted at in the Old Testament.

Dead Sea Scrolls

In Palestine one of the greatest archeological discoveries of our time has been the finding of the Dead Sea Scrolls. At the foot of a rugged cliff, on a whitish-brown terrace looking down toward the Dead Sea, is a place known today as Khirbet Qumran (Ruins of Qumran). Sometime during the latter half of the second century B.C. a community of Essenes separated themselves from orthodox Judaism of Jerusalem and moved to the site. By the spring of 31 B.C. a sizable community had grown up there. It was destroyed by an earthquake, the effects of which I was able to see in the ruins when I visited there in the 1970s. After the earthquake, the site remained uninhabited for a time; but finally the Essenes returned and repaired the buildings, adding some new construction.

About A.D. 68, the Qumran community was destroyed again, this time by the Romans during their campaign in Judea to quell the first Jewish revolt. The members of the community fled, hiding their precious library in nearby caves. Valuable scrolls were wrapped in linen and placed in earthenware jars in what is known today as Cave 1. The mouth of the cave was then sealed with rocks. This library was probably first uncovered in the eighth century, when most of the books were taken to Jerusalem and subsequently lost.

One day in 1947 a young Bedouin, Muhammad Adah-Dhib, was searching for his lost goat in the hills and cliffs behind Khirbet Qumran. In one cliff he noticed a strangely placed hole which seemed to lead into a cave. When he threw a stone into the cave, the boy was surprised to hear the familiar sound of pottery being broken. This aroused Muhammad's curiosity. He pulled himself up to the small cave entrance and peered in. He saw several large, wide-necked jars. Being afraid to enter the cave alone, he returned to the Bedouin camp. Next day he returned to the cave with an older friend. The two squeezed their way through an opening and found several two-foot-high earthenware jars. Later they tried to sell the scrolls they found in those jars to an antiquities dealer in Bethlehem for $56. The dealer was not interested, not realizing that in a few years just five of those eleven scrolls would bring the fabulous price of $250,000 and, of course, today they are considered priceless. Two of the scrolls proved to be Hebrew manuscripts of the book of Isaiah, older by a thousand years than any Old Testament Hebrew manuscripts previously known. It is generally agreed that at least one of these scrolls was written about the second century B.C.

The scroll that seems somewhat older than the other contains the complete text of the book of Isaiah. The second scroll is written in beautiful handwriting by a more experienced scribe, but unfortunately, it is only fragmentary.

These scrolls demonstrate that our present Bible text of Isaiah has come down to us practically unchanged since the time of Christ and before. They also present impressive evidence that the book of Isaiah was the work of just one author instead of two, as is so often claimed, for there is no evidence in either scroll that Isaiah ever existed as two separate books or as the work of two different authors. It seems to have been regarded as a single unit, the work of one author centuries before Christ.

Scrolls or pieces of scrolls have been found in ten other caves since that time, giving the scholarly world nearly 100,000 jigsaw pieces of text to assemble. They are said to represent 870 distinct scrolls, 220 of which are biblical scrolls. They represent every book of the Old Testament except Esther.

The great thrill to the student of prophecy regarding the study of the scrolls comes from the discovery of the fact that Bible prophecy has been verified and reaffirmed. That is because the Messianic prophecies of Isaiah have been shown to have been written in the very form in which we now have them before the time of Christ. The accurate and detailed fulfillment of these Messianic proph-

ecies in the life of Christ not only provides evidence that
He is the Son of God and Saviour of the world but demonstrates the truth and reliability of other prophecies given
by God in the Bible.

The Walls of Jericho

One more dramatic contribution that archeology is
making to the trustworthiness of the Bible is found in
current attempts to recheck the data from Jericho. In the
1960s when I was teaching biblical archeology at Pacific
Union College, Kathleen Kenyon from the British School
of Archaeology had just finished a series of excavations at
Jericho. She decided that the fall of Jericho as portrayed
in the Bible was wrong, because there was no settlement
on that site when the Israelites entered Canaan. This became the standard "gospel" among archeologists who decided that Kenyon was right and the former excavator,
John Garstang, was wrong. Garstang startled the Christian world after his excavations from 1930 to 1936. He
found fallen walls and a burned royal palace that fitted
the Bible description of the destruction of Jericho at the
time the Israelites began to occupy Canaan.

Recently, "Another scholar, Bryant Wood, traveled to
Liverpool, Paris, and Jerusalem to examine Garstang's
old pottery bags that are still stored in those places.
Kenyon's assertion that there was no occupation of Jericho in the time of Joshua was based on her reading of
pottery. Wood criticized her pottery reading on three
counts: (1) she paid too much attention to imported painted
pottery; (2) she paid too little attention to unpainted lo-
cally made pottery; and (3) she missed what painted pottery there was because she did not examine Garstang's
pottery bags in detail and because she did not dig in the
palace. Imported painted wares were luxury goods and
thus were found by Garstang in the palace. Since Garstang

had already excavated the palace, Kenyon could only excavate adjacent to it, and the houses there were more normal, ordinary homes that did not contain luxury goods.

"The problem now is this: everybody admits that the final destruction of Jericho was a massive event that fits the character of the Israelite destruction there, if the pottery date is correct. Kenyon says the pottery date is not correct; Garstang and Wood say that the pottery date is correct" (William H. Shea, "How Shall We Understand the Bible?" *Ministry*, March 1996, 12).

Many scholars now side in with that description which marvelously corroborates the Bible. If archeologists would take the Bible more seriously than they do, they would have much superior presuppositions on which to build and better understand what God tells us happened in the past.

Yes, the stones are crying out in support of inspired Scripture!

How Jesus Dealt With Those Trying to Silence His Message

"Never before had the world seen such a triumphal procession. It was not like that of the earth's famous conquerors. No train of mourning captives, as trophies of kingly valor, made a feature of that scene. But about the Saviour were the glorious trophies of His labors of love for sinful man. There were the captives whom He had rescued from Satan's power, praising God for their deliverance. The blind whom He had restored to sight were leading the way. The dumb whose tongues He had loosed shouted the loudest hosannas. . . . Lazarus, whose body had seen corruption in the grave, but who now rejoiced in the strength of glorious manhood, led the beast on which the Saviour rode.

"Many Pharisees witnessed the scene, and, burning with envy and malice, sought to turn the current of popular feeling. With all their authority they tried to silence the people; but their appeals and threats only increased the enthusiasm. They feared that this multitude, in the strength of their numbers, would make Jesus king. As a last resort they pressed through the crowd to where the Saviour was, and accosted Him with reproving and threatening words: 'Master, rebuke Thy disciples.' They declared that such noisy demonstrations were unlawful, and would not be permitted by the authorities. But they were silenced by the reply of Jesus, 'I tell you that, if these should hold their peace, the stones would immediately cry out.' That scene of triumph was of God's own appointing. It had been foretold by the prophet. . . . Had men failed to carry out His plan, He would have given a voice to the inanimate stones, and they would have hailed His Son with acclamations of praise. . . . Before the day is done, another testimony is borne to Christ. . . .

"The procession is about to descend the Mount of Olives, it is intercepted by the rulers. They inquire the cause of the tumultuous rejoicing. As they question, "Who is this?" the disciples, filled with the spirit of inspiration, answer this question. In eloquent strains they repeat the prophecies concerning Christ:

"Adam will tell you, It is the seed of the woman that shall bruise the serpent's head.

"Ask Abraham, he will tell you, It is Melchizedek King of Salem, King of Peace. Gen. 14:18.

"Jacob will tell you, He is Shiloh of the tribe of Judah.

"Isaiah will tell you, 'Immanuel,' 'Wonderful, Counselor, The mighty God, The everlasting Father, The Prince of Peace.' Isa. 7:14; 9:6.

"Jeremiah will tell you, The Branch of David, 'the Lord our Righteousness.' Jer. 23:6.

"Daniel will tell you, He is the Messiah.

"Hosea will tell you, He is 'the Lord God of hosts; the Lord is His memorial.' Hosea 12:5.

"John the Baptist will tell you, He is 'the Lamb of God, which taketh away the sin of the world.' John 1:29.

"The great Jehovah has proclaimed from His throne, 'This is My beloved Son.' Matt. 3:17.

We, His disciples, declare, This is Jesus, the Messiah, the Prince of life, the Redeemer of the world.

And the prince of the powers of darkness acknowledges Him, saying, 'I know thee who thou art, the Holy One of God.' Mark 1:24 (*The Desire of Ages*, 572-578).

Chapter 7

TIMELY INTERPRETATIONS

Many years ago a man called Doc Noss found several million dollars' worth of gold bricks—at least, that's what he claimed. Doc, part Cheyenne Indian, was an agile fellow. He told any who would listen that during an outing he found the gold at the bottom of a deep cavern in the Umbrillo Basin area of New Mexico. Along with the gold, Doc said, he saw twenty-seven human skeletons tied to posts.

But times have changed. The Umbrillo Basin section of New Mexico is now part of the United States Army's White Sands Missile Range. Rumors of the gold kept cropping up, but the army considered the story a hoax and refused explorers entry into the area. Finally, a Florida based group known as Expedition Unlimited was able to obtain approval for a search. They were not only determined to search for that gold but had seventy-five thousand dollars to invest in the project. Norman Scott, the leader of the group, persuaded the army to suspend all activity on the range for ten days, giving them time to make a thorough and well-organized search of the area.

The lure of gold attracts certain kinds of individuals. Joe Newman, a carpet salesman from El Paso, Texas, put forward a claim that any gold found there belonged by right to the Apache Indians and worked out an arrangement with the tribe whereby he would receive a cut for representing their interests.

Jesse James II, grandson of the notorious outlaw, asserted that his grandfather, Jesse James, was not killed but went underground and buried his loot in the Umbrillo Basin area.

Tony Tally, an elderly member of the expedition team, insisted that he had actually helped Doc Noss bury 110 bars of gold.

Urged on by Doc's widow, the team searched during the allotted ten days, plus an additional three that the longsuffering army allowed. Using metal detectors, ground radar, and all the modern instruments available, they did discover many unknown tunnels and caverns. But no gold.

At the end of thirteen days the disappointed members of the team went their separate ways. Some are still convinced, however, that millions, perhaps billions, of dollars worth of gold are still there—somewhere.

As this incident illustrates, those who search for hidden treasure are often disappointed. But those who continue to put forth the necessary time and effort seeking for the treasure hidden in the Word of God will *always* find it. In God's Word is found unquestionable, inexhaustible wisdom that originated in the infinite mind. However, because this wisdom often lies buried beneath the rubbish of human wisdom and tradition, we must perseveringly search for it.

The Language Problem

Since the Tower of Babel there has been an astounding proliferation of languages and dialects. Languages also are in a constant process of change. This presents two enormous challenges. The first is that of carefully comparing the versions and translations you have in order to discover which best present the meaning of the original languages. The second is the challenge to fulfill Christ's commission by providing the Word of God in every "tongue."

Most of the Old Testament was written in what now is known as ancient Hebrew. A small portion was written in Aramaic. The New Testament was written in *koine* or colloquial Greek as opposed to the classical Greek used by writers of that time. Although the Bible was still read in Hebrew in the synagogues in the time of Christ, Aramaic had become the common language of the Jewish people. Aramaic was the language Jesus spoke. Bible translations began in the third century B.C. when the Hebrew Old Testament was translated into Greek. Near the end of the second century A.D., the New Testament was translated into Syriac (a form of Aramaic), into Latin, and for the believers of Upper Egypt, into Coptic. By 1995 the Bible, or portions of it, had been translated into 2,123 languages.

The Holy Spirit is as actively involved in the work of translation as He was in the initial writing of the Scriptures. "From the beginning, God has been working by His Holy Spirit through human instrumentalities for the accomplishment of His purpose in behalf of the fallen race. This was manifest in the lives of the patriarchs. To the church in the wilderness also, in the time of Moses, God gave His 'good Spirit to instruct them.' Nehemiah 9:20. And in the days of the apostles He wrought mightily for His church through the agency of the Holy Spirit. The same power that sustained the patriarchs, that gave Caleb and Joshua faith and courage, and that made the work of the apostolic church effective, has upheld God's faithful children in every succeeding age. It was through the power of the Holy Spirit that during the Dark Ages the Waldensian Christians helped to prepare the way for the Reformation. It was the same power that made successful the efforts of the noble men and women who pioneered the way for the establishment of modern missions and for the translation of the Bible into the languages and dialects of all nations and peoples" (*The Acts of the Apostles*, 53).

Today the world abounds in Bibles. There are exceptions in certain areas, but for most of us Bibles are readily available. When we were missionaries in Japan, my wife and I studied Japanese and advanced to the point where we were able to read the Japanese Bible pretty well. But our Japanese friends would tease us by telling us that when we read the English Bible we were shaking our heads *No*, for our writing goes from left to right across the page. In the Japanese Bible the characters begin at the top of the page on the right hand side and are read down, so it appears that the reader of the Japanese Bible is nodding *Yes*.

Reading the Bible in another language gives us insights into meanings we may not perceive in our native language. Because the culture and customs of Bible lands was Semitic or Oriental, we learned many things during our years in Japan that Westerners usually do not have the privilege of discovering if they do not travel overseas. The careful Bible student also has the advantage of being able to study the Bible in its original languages and in many modern translations and versions. But because these vary in quality and accuracy, we must become knowledgeable about how to select and use them.

In addition, there are many fine helps available that give us insights to the Scriptures. Bible dictionaries and commentaries, such as the *Seventh-day Adventist Bible Commentary*, are very helpful. Volume 8 of the commentary set is the *SDA Bible Dictionary,* which is an invaluable aid to understanding names, people, geography, and other aspects that contribute to background study. Helpful to those not familiar with Greek and Hebrew is *Young's*

Analytical Concordance, which relates the English word in each case to the biblical language term from which it is translated.

As Seventh-day Adventists, we are blessed with the last-day gift of prophecy. God gave us this gift because He knew that Satan would be at work in the end time to do all he can to confuse the church on the question of revelation and interpretation. What Ellen White predicted is now evident in the pluralistic emphasis on the part of many in the church. There are three basic purposes of this gift: (1) to lead us to the Bible, (2) to help us understand the Bible, and (3) to help us know how to apply Bible principles to daily living.

The Question of Versions

Many cling to the *King James Version* as the most authoritative Bible. All of us treat it as being a truly majestic version. But we need to admit that for some, its language is archaic, obscure, and difficult to understand.

To illustrate this last point, in the back of one of my King James Versions of the Bible is a glossary that lists 454 words that have changed meaning or fallen out of general use since that Bible was first published in 1611. Some samples follow. Why not indicate after each word listed what you think it means; then check the answers at the end of the chapter.

1. affect
2. check
3. clouts
4. fat
5. fray
6. let
7. neesings
8. ouches
9. prevent
10. sith

In spite of the difficulty we sometimes have in understanding the language of the Bible and its cultural setting, many of the incidents recorded are among the best-loved stories of humankind; and the Bible, whichever version you use, still is one of the most-used and popular books there is. Why? Isn't it because it's full of human-interest stories, actual case histories, and real-life situations with real-life people facing the same kinds of problems, frustrations, and decisions that we face today and finding their answers and the way through their problems in God's revealed will?

Stop and think. Where would you go to find the comforting story of a seemingly innocent man who unjustly suffered all kinds of trouble but never gave up his basic faith in the Lord? Of course, Job was discouraged and grumbled and complained at times, but he still ultimately clung to his faith in God.

Where would you go to find an account of a young man separated from his family ties and all that meant everything to him, unjustly accused and imprisoned, yet standing so firmly for his God and his beliefs that he was at last called to minister to the needs of an entire nation and did so most effectively?

Where can you find more thrilling true stories than these? Where else can you find such inspirational material to help you develop a strong confidence in God? Comparing different versions can aid in Bible study, giving you a broader understanding of what the words actually mean. But we must be careful not to be misled by some of the modern translations that are slanted toward a faulty agenda.

It is your privilege to decide how you will answer for yourself the question of what to do about the use of modern versions. You also need to determine whether there will be some advantage to you in learning enough of the basics of biblical languages to be able to gain some extra insights in Bible study.

"Timely Interpretative" Translations

The term "timely interpretative translations" implies that God is sometimes ambiguous, sometimes equivocates, and sometimes seems to do that which contradicts what has been taught in other portions of the Bible. But we can be thankful that God is *not* evasive and that His infallible authority is beyond such things as political correctness and other cultural twentieth-century attempts to update the Bible! Those engaged in such attempts to "improve" the revelation of God try to tell God what He should have said to make Himself culturally acceptable today. But we can rest in full confidence that in His Word He says exactly what He wants to say.

Because the Bible did not employ modern scientific vocabulary or cultural understandings, some take it upon themselves to make kindly corrections. That is not our business. God prepared a book that was intended to be understood and accepted by people of all backgrounds and to be relevant in every age. The Bible makes no distinction between rules of faith and practice on one hand and scientific and historical matters on the other. It provides for all who study its sacred pages an accurate and clear understanding of the divine will for us. Because God changes not and His Word stands forever, we have the assurance that we can make the Bible the bedrock of our understanding and our faith.

Answers to Obscure KJV Words:
1. *affect*: to desire earnestly, seek after (Gal. 4:17).
2. *check*: reproof, rebuke (Job 20:3).
3. *clouts*: cloth patches, rags (Jer. 38:11).
4. *fat*: a vat, vessel (Joel 2:24; 3:15).

5. *fray*: to frighten (Deut. 28:26; Jer. 7:33).
6. *let*: to hinder, prevent (Exod. 5:4; Romans 1:13).
7. *neesings*: Sneezings (Job 41:18).
8. *ouches*: sockets in which precious stones are set (Exod. 28:11).
9. *prevent*: to do or come before, to anticipate (Ps. 18:5; 1 Thess. 4:15).
10. *sith*: since (Ezek. 35:6).

How Jesus Dealt With Confusion and False Interpretation

"The teachers of Israel were not sowing the seed of the word of God. Christ's work as a teacher of truth was in marked contrast to that of the rabbis of His time. They dwelt upon traditions, upon human theories and speculations. Often that which man had taught and written about the word, they put in place of the word itself. Their teaching had no power to quicken the soul. The subject of Christ's teaching and preaching was the word of God. He met questioners with a plain, 'It is written.' 'What saith the Scriptures?' 'How readest thou?' At every opportunity, when an interest was awakened by either friend or foe, He sowed the seed of the word. He who is the way, the Truth, and the Life, Himself the living Word, points to the Scriptures, saying, 'They are they which testify of Me." And 'beginning at Moses and all the prophets,' He opened to His disciples 'in all the Scriptures the things concerning Himself.' John 5:39; Luke 24:27.

"Christ's servants are to do the same work. In our day, as of old, the vital truths of God's word are set aside for human theories and speculations. Many professed ministers of the gospel do not accept the whole Bible as the inspired word. One wise man rejects one portion; another questions another part. They set up their judgment as superior to the word; and the Scripture which they do teach rests upon their own authority. Its divine authenticity is destroyed. Thus the seeds of infidelity are sown broadcast; for the people become confused and know not what to believe. There are many beliefs that the mind has no right to entertain. In the days of Christ the rabbis put a forced, mystical construction upon many portions of Scripture. Because the plain teaching of God's word condemned their practices, they tried to destroy its force. The same thing is done today. The word of God is made to appear mysterious and obscure in order to excuse transgression of His law. Christ rebuked these practices in His day. He taught that the word of God was to be understood by all. He pointed to the Scriptures as of unquestionable authority, and we should do the same. The Bible is to be presented as the word of the infinite God, as the end of all controversy and the foundation of all faith."

"The Bible has been robbed of its power, and the results are seen in a lowering of the tone of spiritual life. In the sermons from many pulpits of today there is not that divine manifestation which awakens the conscience and brings life to the soul. The hearers can not say, 'Did not our heart burn within us, while He talked with us by the way, and while He opened to us the Scriptures?' Luke 24:32. There are many who are crying out for the living God, longing for the divine presence. Philosophical theories or literary essays, however brilliant, cannot satisfy the heart. The assertions and inventions of men are of no value. Let the word of God speak to the people. Let those who have heard only traditions and human theories and maxims hear the voice of Him whose word can renew the soul unto everlasting life. . . .

"Instead of discussing erroneous theories, or seeking to combat the opponents of the gospel, follow the example of Christ. Let fresh truths from God's treasure house flash into life. 'Preach the word.' 'Sow beside all waters.' 'Be instant in season, out of season.' 'He that hath My word, let him speak My word faithfully. . . .' " 2 Tim. 4:2; Isa. 32:20; Jer. 23:28 (*Christ's Object Lessons*, 38-40).

Chapter 8

SEVENTH-DAY
"FAD"-VENTISTS

Second Timothy 4:3, 4 indicates that many in the last days will turn from sound biblical interpretation but will "heap to themselves teachers, having itching ears; and they shall turn away their ears from truth, and shall be turned unto fables." Notice that first of all they "will not endure sound doctrine." Many of these will turn against the clear teachings of the Bible because they think of them as being too restrictive and too authoritarian. When they turn from the solid basis of their faith they become "FAD"-ventists, jumping from one sensational teaching to another.

One of the strange things about their turning away from truth seems to be that they flock to anyone coming up with sensational and way-out teachings. But they are not interested in listening to careful interpretations on the part of teachers who accept the Bible as being the Word of God and who base their Adventist belief on the firm platform of biblical doctrine.

One example of this kind of fadism is seen in the various groups who have been focusing on Jubilee years as an indication of when the Lord will come. They do so in spite of Ellen White's clear statement. After describing the angel of Revelation 10 as proclaiming that time shall be no longer, she adds: "This time, which the angel declares with a solemn oath, is not the end of this world's history, neither of probationary time, but of prophetic time, which should precede the advent of our Lord. That is, the people will not have another message upon definite time. After this period of time, reaching from 1842 to 1844, there can be no definite tracing of the prophetic time. The longest reckoning reaches to the autumn of 1844" (Ellen G. White Comments, *SDA Bible Commentary*, 7:971).

The key to dealing with this and similar problems is the way we approach Scripture. The only safe foundation principle for studying God's Word is the Bible itself. Not only is the Bible its own best interpreter, but its total context and philosophy must give us the key to understanding the portions of Scripture we study.

The late Dr. Gerhard Hasel developed nine principles of interpretation that we will use as an outline for this chapter (Lee J. Gugliotto, "The Crisis of Exegesis," *Ministry,* March 1996, 8). I will then add one of my own that I believe is helpful in putting them all together.

1. The Bible is its own best expositor. Because the true author is the Holy Spirit, we need to allow Him to say what He wants to say by putting together what He says in one place with what He teaches in other passages. Instead of criticizing the contents of the Bible, we must surrender to its authority and allow the Bible to interpret the Bible.

2. The Bible must not be interpreted on the basis of a principle derived from a selected part of Scripture at the expense of the entire message of the Bible. One example is the parable of the rich man and Lazarus (see Luke 16:19-31). Whereas parables teach moral principles, they are not intended to be literal. Sections in this parable that contradict what the rest of the Bible teaches include: conversation between those in heaven and hell, all the saved fitting into Abraham's bosom, and the righteous watching the constant suffering and punishment of the wicked. Jesus used a common misconception of the Jews to show that riches are not necessarily a sign of God's favor as they believed and that poverty is not a punishment for sin. Yet it is the Bible and not human judgment that distinguishes between that which is of universal application and that which is limited.

3. *Each passage must be studied within its immediate and larger contexts.* Context does not mean just a few verses preceding and following a passage. Context often includes the entire chapter or a larger portion of a book. The ultimate context is the entire Bible.

4. *Texts (scriptures) must be compared with other texts (scriptures) by the same author.* For instance, those who understand that Paul's expression "to be absent from the body, and to be present with the Lord" in 2 Corinthians 5:6, 8 refers to immortality can find the true meaning explained in the context of verses 1-9. He contrasts our being in our earthly tabernacle (our bodies) with the building of God—being at home with the body and absent from the Lord versus being present with the Lord "that mortality might be swallowed up of life." Undoubtedly, Paul was yearning for the second coming of Christ (Titus 2:13) at which time "the last trumpet shall sound, and the dead shall be raised incorruptible" (1 Cor. 15:53, 54). In verse 51 Paul speaks of death as a "sleep." He also calls "death" a "sleep" in 1 Thessalonians 4:13 and 5:10. When you put these and several other passages from Paul together, you understand that when a righteous person dies, that person sleeps in death until Jesus comes and the trumpet sounds, calling His people from their graves. Then, and not until then, will mortals put on immortality.

"The evidence of truth is in the Scripture itself. One scripture is the key to unlock other scriptures. The rich and hidden meaning is unfolded by the Holy Spirit of God, making plain the word to our understanding" (*Fundamentals of Christian Education*, 390).

5. *Difficult texts on a given subject must be explained on the basis of those that are plain or clear on the same subject and not vice versa.* On issues that still need some clarification in understanding, we need to search for the weight of evidence. "God does not compel men to give up their unbelief. Before them are light and darkness, truth and error. It is for them to decide which they will accept. The human mind is endowed with power to discriminate between right and wrong. God designs that men shall not decide from impulse, but from weight of evidence, carefully comparing scripture with scripture. Had the Jews laid by their prejudice and compared written prophecy with the facts characterizing the life of Jesus, they would have perceived a beautiful harmony between the prophecies and their fulfillment in the life and ministry of the lowly Galilean" (*The Desire of Ages,* 458).

6. *The unity of the Bible must be maintained.* There is a unity throughout the Bible that encompasses diversity without contradiction. When Jesus walked with two disciples on the road to Emmaus, He did His best to enlighten them on His mission, death, and resurrection by "beginning at Moses and all the prophets, he expounded unto them in all the scriptures the things concerning himself" (Luke 24:27). What they needed was to study every text in the Old Testament, as well as what Christ preached, to discover how the Bible presents a unified picture. Think about this for a moment: Is it possible to express a belief in the unity and authority of the Scriptures but to deny that position by adopting false hermeneutical principles that lead to erroneous conclusions?

7. *Exegetical possibilities should not be used to establish biblical teaching, church doctrine, and practice.* One

example of an exegetical point that has bothered some church members in recent years is the question of whether the translation "virgin" or "young woman" is correct. Some have even gone so far as to deny Christ's virgin birth. The Hebrew word *'Almah* specifically denotes a young woman of marriageable age and in the light of a double application of prophecy could apply to a young woman giving birth in Isaiah's day as well as Christ's virgin birth. There is a specific term for "virgin" in Hebrew, but if it were used here it would nullify the initial application to the fulfillment of the sign God gave Ahaz. The "prophetess" bore a promised son whom Ahaz must have recognized because of the timing involved. The fact that a later inspired writer realized that the application to a "virgin" in Matthew 1:19-24 and Luke 1:26-38 supports the virgin birth makes it clear that God intended a dual fulfillment of the Messianic prophecy of Isaiah 7:14.

8. Scriptures that are circumstantial or culturally conditioned and tied to a command or injunction are not necessarily of limited or temporal application. This implies that some can be—but not necessarily so. By carefully and prayerfully applying the hermeneutical principles here being outlined and regarding how other Bible writers apply such passages, we should be able to discover which category applies. Here we must be careful not to be deceived by human preconceptions and conjectures.

"To my ministering brethren I would say, Preach the word. Do not bring to the foundation wood, hay, and stubble,—your own surmisings and speculations, which can benefit no one. Subjects of vital importance are revealed in the Word of God, and these are worthy of our deepest thought. But we are not to search into matters on which God has been silent.

"When questions arise upon which we are uncertain,

let us ask, What saith the Scripture? And if the Scripture is silent upon the question at issue, let it not be made the subject of discussion. Let those who wish for something new, seek for that newness of life resulting from the new birth. Let them purify their souls by obeying the truth, and act in harmony with the instruction that Christ has given" (*Gospel Workers*, 314).

9. Some New Testament texts are both contextual commands (injunctions) and normative principles, expressed by appeal to (a) creation, (b) the law, and (c) the argument from the Fall. How can immoral people develop moral norms? That's like turning the bank over to the robbers to run. Only the God of love and justice has the right and the ability to give us commands that reveal His greatness, goodness, and love. All His commands are enablings. The Lord who loves us far more than anyone else can love us (far more than we love ourselves) knows what is best for us and wants us to have that which is far better than we would normally choose. Actually, it is impossible for us to understand and choose until we have been enlightened by the Holy Spirit. (This point is illustrated by the Pharisees' minimal obedience compared to Jesus' understanding of the principles involved, for which there are no maximums. See Matt. 5:21-48.)

10. The one I wish to add is implied above. It is clear that *we must check carefully the points being studied in the light of the overall view—the theme of all revelation.* The great controversy theme and the plan of salvation are the center around which all other truths cluster. This principle will be discussed in detail in chapter 12.

Within the context of point 10, we need to emphasize the Bible's positive outlook and assurance of victory for Christ's people. Wilbur Wright arrived in France in 1908 intent on demonstrating the superiority of his flying machine over the experimental models being produced there.

Understandably, there was quite a bit of hostility toward him as the French were committed to defending the claims of priority being made by their own aviators.

Wilbur first exhibited the flying ability of his craft at LeMans on August 8 of that year. When a catapult shot him thirty feet into the air to begin his flight, the large crowd of spectators gasped with surprise. They were used to seeing long and often unsuccessful takeoffs.

Then his flying machine dipped its left wing sharply and banked for a turn. The crowd panicked. This was the first they had seen or even heard of an airplane turning like that, and they thought Wilbur was going to crash. Up until now the few flights that had taken place in France involved wide, jerky, level-winged circles as the only means of turning.

As Wilbur continued to gracefully circle the grandstand, the frightened gasps of the spectators turned into wild, enthusiastic cheering. When he gently landed on the field after his performance, the shouting, applauding mob thronged about the plane. Everyone was trying to shake his hand at once. Even the French aviators present acknowledged that the Wright brothers had come up with the best approach to manned flight and a greatly superior flying machine. Something better speaks for itself. But too often in our approach to sharing and in our personal interpretation of Scripture we leave the impression that what we're suggesting is BITTER rather than BETTER. "Don't do this and don't do that" are popular expressions, but they do not attract people. How much better to show that what God has to offer is something infinitely better. For witness to be effective, we must demonstrate that we have found God's something better in our own lives.

How Jesus Broke Through Barriers of Formalism and Tradition

"In the midst of the feast, when the excitement concerning Him was at its height, He entered the court of the temple in the presence of the multitude. Because of His absence from the feast, it had been urged that He dared not place Himself in the power of the priests and rulers. All were surprised at His presence. Every voice was hushed. All wondered at the dignity and courage of His bearing in the midst of powerful enemies who were thirsting for His life.

"Standing thus, the center of attraction to that vast throng, Jesus addressed them as no man had ever done. His words showed a knowledge of the laws and institutions of Israel, of the sacrificial service and the teachings of the prophets, far exceeding that of the priests and rabbis. He broke through the barriers of formalism and tradition. The scenes of the future life seemed outspread before Him. As one who beheld the Unseen, He spoke of the earthly and the heavenly, the human and the divine, with positive authority. His words were most clear and convincing; and again, as at Capernaum, the people were astonished at His teaching; 'for His word was with power.' Luke 4:32. Under a variety of representations He warned His hearers of the calamity that would follow all who rejected the blessings He came to bring them. He had given them every possible proof that He came forth from God, and made every possible effort to bring them to repentance. He would not be rejected and murdered by His own nation if He could save them from the guilt of such a deed.

"All wondered at His knowledge of the law and the prophecies; and the question passed from one to another, 'How knoweth this Man letters, having never learned?' No one was regarded as qualified to be a religious teacher unless he had studied in the rabbinical schools, and both Jesus and John the Baptist had been represented as ignorant because they had not received this training. . . .

"Day after day He taught the people, until the last, 'that great day of the feast.' The morning of this day found the people wearied from the long season of festivity. Suddenly Jesus lifted up His voice, in tones that rang through the courts of the temple: "If any man thirst, let him come unto Me, and drink. He that believeth on Me, as the scripture hath said, out of his belly shall flow rivers of living water." The condition of the people made this appeal very forcible. They had been engaged in a continued scene of pomp and festivity, their eyes had been dazzled with light and color, and their ears regaled with the richest music; but there had been nothing in all this round of ceremonies to meet the wants of the spirit, nothing to satisfy the thirst of the soul for that which perishes not. Jesus invited them to come and drink of the fountain of life. . . .

"The priest had that morning performed the ceremony which commemorated the smiting of the rock in the wilderness. That rock was a symbol of Him who by His death would cause living streams of salvation to flow to all who are athirst. Christ's words were the water of life. . . .

"That sudden cry, 'If any man thirst,' startled them from their sorrowful meditation, and as they listened to the words that followed, their minds kindled with a new hope. The Holy Spirit presented the symbol before them until they saw in it the offer of the priceless gift of salvation" (*The Desire of Ages,* 452-454).

Chapter 9

AN UNFAILING GUIDE FOR THE LAST DAYS

People who have trouble understanding the book of Daniel might take some courage from the fact that Daniel himself had a hard time understanding that which was revealed to him. His major problem was his fixation on his people being released soon from their Babylonian captivity. What did the 1260- and the 2300-year prophecies have to do with his mind-set at that time?

Because these prophecies have been fulfilled, we now realize that we are living in the end time. Many people don't want to know that. They are hoping that everything will go on just as it is, although some of the more perceptive will admit that what is going on is far from ideal.

On top of that and behind it all there's Satan. His self-interest demands that he keep as many people as possible from getting ready for Christ to come. Apparently he's doing a good job in the light of the fact that few among earth's population are preparing seriously for the end of the world.

In Daniel's case it is not surprising that the prophet could not understand well what was going to happen 2,500 years after his time. God explained this carefully to him in Daniel 12, promising that he would "stand in his lot"— would be understood—when the time came for his "little book" to be unsealed.

Daniel Standing in His Lot

What it meant for Daniel to "stand in his lot" is explained by Ellen White in the following references: "In his vision of the last days Daniel inquired, 'O my Lord, what shall be the end of these things?' And he said, 'Go thy way, Daniel: for the words are closed up and sealed till the time of the end. Many shall be purified, and made white, and tried; but the wicked shall do wickedly: and none of the wicked shall understand; but the wise shall understand. . . . Blessed is he that waiteth, and cometh to the thousand three hundred and five and thirty days. But go thou thy way till the end be: for thou shalt rest, and stand in thy lot at the end of the days' [Dan. 12:8-13]. Daniel has been standing in his lot since the seal was removed and the light of truth has been shining upon his visions. He stands in his lot, bearing the testimony which was to be understood at the end of the days" (Ellen White, *Sermons and Talks,* 1:225).

Another reference that enlarges on this particular understanding of "stand in his lot" states: "Honored by men with the responsibilities of state and with the secrets of kingdoms bearing universal sway, Daniel was honored by God as His ambassador, and was given many revelations of the mysteries of ages to come. His wonderful prophecies, as recorded by him in chapters 7 to 12 of the book bearing his name, were not fully understood even by the prophet himself; but before his life labors closed, he was given the blessed assurance that 'at the end of the days'—in the closing period of this world's history—he would again be permitted to stand in his lot and place" (*Conflict and Courage*, 254).

When is the time for Daniel to "stand in his lot"? "After these seven thunders uttered their voices, the injunction comes to John as to Daniel in regard to the little book: 'Seal up those things which the seven thunders uttered.'

These relate to future events which will be disclosed in their order. Daniel shall stand in his lot at the end of the days. John sees the little book unsealed. Then Daniel's prophecies have their proper place in the first, second, and third angels' messages to be given to the world. The unsealing of the little book was the message in relation to time" (Ellen G. White Comments, *SDA Bible Commentary*, 7:971).

The message that relates to time is the last of the Bible time prophecies—the 2300 years that ended in 1844. Daniel's prophecy concerning the book being unsealed reached down to the time when the three angels' messages were given to the world.

A comment on the prophecy of Revelation 10 also adds to our understanding of Daniel 12. "The mighty angel who instructed John was no less a personage than Jesus Christ. Setting His right foot on the sea, and His left upon the dry land, shows the part which He is acting in the closing scenes of the great controversy with Satan. This position denotes His supreme power and authority over the whole earth. The controversy has waxed stronger and more determined from age to age, and will continue to do so, to the concluding scenes when the masterly working of the powers of darkness shall reach their height. Satan, united with evil men, will deceive the whole world and the churches who receive not the love of the truth. But the mighty angel demands attention. He cries with a loud voice. He is to show the power and authority of His voice to those who have united with Satan to oppose the truth. . . . Daniel shall stand in his lot at the end of the days. John sees the little book unsealed. Then Daniel's prophecies have their proper place in the first, second, and third angels' messages to be given to the world. The unsealing of the little book was the message in relation to time" (*Manuscript Releases*, 1:99).

It is God who has unsealed the last time prophecies of

the book of Daniel. We are living in the time when these prophecies are to be understood clearly. Because Satan could not keep the prophecies from being unsealed, he has put a tremendous amount of effort in trying to obscure their meaning by assisting people to come up with all sorts of wild interpretations that have largely drawn Bible students' minds away from the true meaning. Living in the age of Millennium-madness, we recognize that there are more of these contradictory interpretations of prophecy circulating than ever before. How are we going to be able to thread our way through the eschatological fads and falsehoods now sweeping the religions of the world? Under the guidance of the Holy Spirit we must let the Bible explain the Bible without adding our preconceptions. That is why we must pray for the Spirit's guidance every time we open the Bible to study.

Must Get Down on Our Knees

Elder Eric Hare lived on a mission compound when he was not itinerating. One day he heard a great hullabaloo outside where a crowd was gathering. As he ran out, he saw the crowd gathered around a very large female elephant.

"She is hurt, Sahib," one of the group told him.

Elder Hare noticed a wound high on her back where she had been gored in a fight. He called for a ladder and a bucket of disinfectant. Placing the ladder against the elephant's side, he began to climb. Startled, the elephant ran away.

"Can you make her lie down?" Elder Hare asked.

The mahout came close and whispered in her ear. The elephant lowered herself carefully to the ground, groaningly getting down on her knees. Elder Hare was able to reach the wound and swabbed it efficiently then dusted it with antiseptic powder. The elephant seemed to feel better and moved away with the crowd. The fact that her wound could not be treated until she got down on her knees is a good illustration for us of how our wounds of sin cannot be healed by Bible study until we get down on our knees and ask the Spirit to guide us as we open the Book of healing.

"We should come with reverence to the study of the Bible, feeling that we are in the presence of God. All lightness and trifling should be laid aside. While some portions of the word are easily understood, the true meaning of other parts is not so readily discerned. There must be patient study and meditation and earnest prayer. Every student, as he opens the Scriptures, should ask for the enlightenment of the Holy Spirit; and the promise is sure that it will be given" (*Testimonies to Ministers*, 107, 108).

New Light That Contradicts Old Light Is No Light

Chapter 10 deals with principles of prophetic interpretation. But one principle that is important to study at this stage is based on Isaiah 8:20—new light that contradicts old light is NO light. God promises to protect us from devils and false teachers by this most significant test. It implies that we need to be safeguarded by understanding the "old light."

Many times my wife and I and our boys visited the Buddhist temple in Nagano, Japan. The first time we were there we saw the prayer tree and a wooden idol that had been worn down by people in search of healing rubbing that part on the idol that corresponded with their illness. Then our priest-guide invited us to walk with him through an underground passage where we could find the "door to heaven." He explained that because it would be very dark, we needed to walk in single file hanging onto the hands of those ahead and behind us. As we followed the guide, we noticed the hallway becoming narrower. But it was too late to turn back. Finally we heard the clanging of the great brass knocker on the "door to heaven" and soon were knocking on it ourselves. A few seconds later we turned a corner into a dimly lighted room and at last stumbled out into bright sunlight. What a difference there is between attempting to get to heaven in the darkness of other religions or of deluded self-interest and the glorious, steady light of the gospel.

In the most perilous time in earth's history, we are only half awake. Now is the time to study Daniel and Revelation. Careful study of these books will bring about a reformation. "The perils of the last days are upon us, and in our work we are to warn the people of the danger they are in. Let not the solemn scenes which prophecy has revealed be left untouched. If our people were half awake, if they realized the nearness of the events portrayed in the Revelation, a reformation would be wrought in our churches, and many more would believe the message. We have no time to lose; God calls upon us to watch for souls as they that must give an account. Advance new principles, and crowd in the clear-cut truth. . . . Let Daniel speak, let the Revelation speak, and tell what is truth. But whatever phase of the subject is presented, uplift Jesus as the center of all hope, 'the Root and the Offspring of David, and the bright and morning Star.'

"We do not go deep enough in our search for truth. Every soul who believes present truth will be brought where he will be required to give a reason of the hope that is in him. The people of God will be called upon to stand before kings, princes, rulers, and great men of the earth, and they must know that they do know what is truth. They must be converted men and women. God can teach you more in one moment by His Holy Spirit than you could learn from the great men of the earth. The universe is looking upon the controversy that is going on upon the earth. At an infinite cost, God has provided for every man an opportunity to know that which will make him wise unto salvation. How eagerly do angels look to see who will avail himself of this opportunity! When a message is presented to God's people, they should not rise up in opposition to it; they should go to the Bible, comparing it with the law and the testimony, and if it does not bear this test, it is not true. God wants our minds to expand. He desires to put His grace upon us. We may have a feast of good things every day, for God can open the whole treasure of heaven to us" (*Testimonies to Ministers*, 118, 119).

Careful Bible study under the guidance of the Holy Spirit is the only way to protect ourselves from fadism, fanaticism, and false prophets today. The Scriptures must be our safeguard. In order for them to be on guard in our lives we must study them daily, urged on by the realization of the wonderful and awesome experiences already beginning to take place as outlined in Bible prophecy.

How Jesus Dealt With Prophetic Misconceptions

"In every page, whether history, or precept, or prophecy, the Old Testament Scriptures are irradiated with the glory of the Son of God. So far as it was of divine institution, the entire system of Judaism was a compacted prophecy of the gospel. To Christ 'give all the prophets witness.' Acts 10:43. From the promise given to Adam, down through the patriarchal line and the legal economy, heaven's glorious light made plain the footsteps of the Redeemer. Seers beheld the Star of Bethlehem, the Shiloh to come, as future things swept before them in mysterious procession. In every sacrifice Christ's death was shown. In every cloud of incense His righteousness ascended. By every jubilee trumpet His name was sounded. In the awful mystery of the holy of holies His glory dwelt.

"The Jews had the Scriptures in their possession, and supposed that in their mere outward knowledge of the word they had eternal life. But Jesus said, 'Ye have not His word abiding in you.' Having rejected Christ in His word, they rejected Him in person. 'Ye will not come to Me,' He said, 'that ye might have life.'

"The Jewish leaders had studied the teachings of the prophets concerning the kingdom of the Messiah; but they had done this, not with a sincere desire to know the truth, but with the purpose of finding evidence to sustain their ambitious hopes. When Christ came in a manner contrary to their expectations, they would not receive Him; and in order to justify themselves, they tried to prove Him a deceiver. When once they had set their feet in this path, it was easy for Satan to strengthen their opposition to Christ. The very words that should have been received as evidence of His divinity were interpreted against Him. Thus they turned the truth of God into a lie, and the more directly the Saviour spoke to them in His works of mercy, the more determined they were in resisting the light" (*The Desire of Ages*, 211, 212).

Chapter 10

NO PRIVATE INTERPRETATION

On a May morning in 1904 Hide (Hee-deh) Kuniya sat in his study behind the tiny Seventh-day Adventist church in Kobe, Japan. As he worked on his translations, Hide thought of his friend, Professor Grainger, who had come to Japan to bring the gospel to Hide's people. After a few years of work, Grainger died. But several young men had accepted his message, and Hide had become an ordained minister.

As he glanced toward the street from his small office in the Kobe church, Hide blinked in surprise. A man dressed in a long white robe and a black stovepipe hat stood at the church signboard, obviously studying it. Hurrying outside, Hide greeted the man. The stranger looked at him blankly. Noting the high cheekbones and getting a better look at the clothes, Hide realized that he was attempting to communicate with a Korean. Motioning to the Korean gentleman to wait for him, Hide rushed into his study and soon was back with paper, ink, and brush. The Japanese and Koreans do not speak the same language, but they use many of the same Chinese characters as part of their written language.

Hide wrote out his name and told a little about his work. The Korean's face broke into a wide grin as he answered the message. In order to catch the next ship to Hawaii, he had to lay over in Kobe for thirty days. In the meantime he wanted to know more about "The Seventh-day Sabbath-keeping Jesus' Second Coming Church" as it was called in the characters on the sign.

How the brush flew on the paper, and how quickly the graceful Chinese characters told the story of God's love. The next day You Un Hyun returned with a friend, Soon Heung Cho, who was just as eager for truth as he was. Before their ship sailed, these two Koreans had been baptized, the first Koreans to become Seventh-day Adventists.

Isn't it wonderful how God can enable people to communicate the gospel in spite of language barriers? In our attempt to communicate the gospel, we run into many kinds of obstacles—some self-imposed and even some that apparently are created by the devil.

Even when people speak the same language there are barriers that stand in the way of effective communication. On the way to Emmaus after the resurrection, Jesus joined two of His followers who were prevented from recognizing Him. After drawing from them the fact that they were discouraged because their Master's death had shaken their conviction that He was the Messiah, Jesus said, "Oh, how foolish you are, how slow to believe in all that the prophets have said" (Luke 24:25, Phillips). The problem was not that they rejected all the prophecies about Christ but that they had been focusing on those that emphasized setting up His kingdom on earth, while ignoring those that outlined His rejection, suffering, death, and resurrection.

In addition to selective use of prophecies, another common obstacle that many evangelicals have in these days is the lack of understanding of "conditional" prophecies. Many of the Old Testament prophetic statements were contingent on Israel fulfilling the expectations and the role God had placed on them in the establishment of Christ's kingdom. Instead, when He came in the time appointed, they rejected Him because He did not fulfill the role of world king and physical deliverer of the people that they thought He should, based on their understanding of Old Testament prophecies.

Seven principles of prophetic interpretation need to be distinguished from the general rules of biblical interpretation outlined in chapter 8, although several are similar. Here we deal in a more limited field—the rules of interpretation that are useful in accurately understanding events written long ago for the blessing and admonition of those living in the last days. Along with the list of the seven principles outlined below, specific prophecies will be used when necessary to demonstrate how these rules apply.

1. Both Daniel and Revelation contain several series of often-parallel outline prophecies that unfold an unbroken sequence of events leading up to the establishment of the eternal kingdom of God. For instance, Nebuchadnezzar's dream of the image in Daniel 2 provides an introduction to, as well as an overview of, prophetic sequence. Instead of the image, Daniel 7 uses prophetic beasts that cover a similar outline but give more insights and additional details of what happens—particularly at the time of the pre-Advent judgment. Daniel 8 and 9 begin with more prophetic beasts, even to the extent of naming the next world powers as Medo-Persia and Greece (Dan. 8:20, 21). Because this prophecy was given in the final years of Babylonian power (Dan. 8:1), Babylon was not indicated as it was in Daniel 7. Instead, the focus was upon those kingdoms soon to come. Three time prophecies are introduced in Daniel 7, 8, and 9—the 1260, 2300, and 490 day-years which, in the case of the last two, began with the decree to restore and rebuild Jerusalem in 457 B.C. The last of the great Bible time prophecies ends in

1844 with the opening of the pre-Advent judgment. The prophetic outline concludes with Daniel 11 and 12, which fill in some quite specific details that were not brought out in the earlier outlines.

2. *The focus of these outline prophecies is the perennial conflict between the nations and God's people, between the antichrist and Christ.* Although there will be an increasingly bitter struggle, Christ and His people will be given the victory and a restored dominion over this earth from which every trace of sin has been removed, with the exception of the scars on Christ's body that serve as the eternal reminder of the price of our salvation.

3. *Each distinct series reveals a repetition and further enlargement of certain parts of a previous series, always focusing on redemptive history, specifically on the final conflict of good and evil.* The seven churches, seven seals, and seven trumpets of the first part of Revelation outline aspects of history leading from the first coming of Christ to His second coming. These, in turn, are followed by an overview of the great controversy in chapter 12, along with additional details of last-day events in chapters 13–22, many of which still are to be fulfilled and end with God and His people in the New Jerusalem.

4. *In and through Jesus Christ both the Old and the New Testament apocalyptic prophecies are to be viewed as a general spiritual unity.* When interpreting the New Testament apocalyptic, we must first consider the historical and theological Old Testament context yet recognize the weight of the wider context of both testaments. Because the book of Revelation (which is called the Apocalypse in Greek) refers more than 490 times to the Old Testament, we should seek to discover how the redemptive history and the message of each book finds its culmination in the Apocalypse.

5. It is important to determine, when the data permits, where each prophetic outline series passes the time of the

cross of Christ, because Old Testament terminology and imagery from that point on should receive an interpretation that takes into consideration the message and mission of Christ and the establishment of the church as the new Israel.

6. Old Testament apocalyptic prophecies that have remained unfulfilled generally because of Israel's failure to meet God's conditions will, according to the New Testament, find their fulfillment in the faithful remnant people of Jesus Christ. Many of the prophecies found in the Old Testament books were conditional on Israel fulfilling the requirements necessary to Christ's setting up His eternal kingdom in Jerusalem at the time of His first advent. "If the [Jewish] nation had been faithful to its trust . . . the whole earth would have awaited the coming of the Messiah with eager expectancy. He would have come, He would have died, and would have risen again. Jerusalem would have become a great missionary center (*Christ's Object Lessons*, 232), and the earth would have been set ablaze with the light of truth" (*SDA Bible Commentary*, 4:29, 30). Because the people of Israel never did accept Him in the way that was necessary, "the predictions of national honor and glory . . . could not be fulfilled. Yet, since God's purposes are immutable . . . success must and will come— through Israel after the spirit" (ibid., 34).

7. Although the same prophetic symbol may most often carry the same basic meaning, the specific application of each symbol is to be determined by its own immediate context. The woman representing God's people or His church and the serpent as a symbol of Satan are found both in Genesis and Revelation. On the other hand, the "four winds" of Revelation 7:1 represent the four main points of the compass, whereas winds can also be used as a symbol of war's destruction. It usually symbolizes activity or energy in some form that can only be understood by full attention to the context.

Because we have the "more sure word of prophecy," ours is a living hope in the soon return of Christ (2 Pet. 1:19). Our understanding of prophecy must first be Christ-centered as He is the focus of all prophecy. It must not be "of any private interpretation" (2 Pet. 1:20). Unfortunately, with today's focus on the coming millennium and on new-age religions, an overabundance of strange prophetic interpretations is being promoted throughout the world. Muslim fundamentalism and Buddhist revival are sweeping certain areas. The New Age manifestations present a less stringent form of spiritualism, Zen and Yoga, and are so syncretistic that it becomes difficult to find a true core of belief, let alone a "more sure word of prophecy."

Revelation Seminars have brought a great blessing in the area of prophetic preaching to the church in recent years. Prior to this, "evangelistic numbers" were sneered at by some SDA teachers, and even evangelistic meetings were characterized by an ecumenical approach to the point that prophetic preaching was either seriously downgraded or misapplied to suit the whims of the interpreter.

The safest guide to applying prophecy accurately is to find applications made by the Holy Spirit in the Bible or in the Spirit of Prophecy. One reason that God puts so much emphasis on the latter is that we are living in the time when prophecies are being fulfilled rapidly. We must have inspired help to understand what is happening, especially now when Satan is striving to deceive the very elect.

How Jesus Dealt With Selective Applications of Prophecy

"As they departed from God, the Jews in a great degree lost sight of the teaching of the ritual service. That service had been instituted by Christ

Himself. In every part it was a symbol of Him; and it had been full of vitality and spiritual beauty. But the Jews lost the spiritual life from their ceremonies, and clung to the dead forms. They trusted to the sacrifices and ordinances themselves, instead of resting upon Him to whom they pointed. In order to supply the place of that which they had lost, the priests and rabbis multiplied requirements of their own; and the more rigid they grew, the less of the love of God was manifested. They measured their holiness by the multitude of their ceremonies, while their hearts were filled with pride and hypocrisy.

"With all their minute and burdensome injunctions, it was an impossibility to keep the law. Those who desired to serve God, and who tried to observe the rabbinical precepts, toiled under a heavy burden. They could find no rest from the accusings of a troubled conscience. Thus Satan worked to discourage the people, to lower their conception of the character of God, and to bring the faith of Israel into contempt. He hoped to establish the claim put forth when he rebelled in heaven,—that the requirements of God were unjust, and could not be obeyed. Even Israel, he declared, did not keep the law.

"While the Jews desired the advent of the Messiah, they had no true conception of His mission. They did not seek redemption from sin, but deliverance from the Romans. They looked for the Messiah to come as a conqueror, to break the oppressor's power, and exalt Israel to universal dominion. Thus the way was prepared for them to reject the Saviour. . . .

"Hatred of the Romans, and national and spiritual pride, led the Jews still to adhere rigorously to their forms of worship. The priests tried to maintain a reputation for sanctity by scrupulous attention to the ceremonies of religion. The people, in their darkness and oppression, and the rulers, thirsting for power, longed for the coming of One who would vanquish their enemies and restore the kingdom to Israel. They had studied the prophecies, but without spiritual insight. Thus they overlooked those scriptures that point to the humiliation of Christ's first advent, and misapplied those that speak of the glory of His second coming. Pride obscured their vision. They interpreted prophecy in accordance with their selfish desires" (*The Desire of Ages*, 29, 30).

Chapter 11

RIGHTLY DIVIDING THE WORD

Many distortions and misunderstandings of the Bible are circulating in scholarly circles today. One reason for these twisted views is that Satan has launched a desperate all-out attack to discredit the Bible and its Author. Another is the explosion of knowledge and information that has come about in the computer age. It is frustrating to the careful Bible scholar to find some way-out positions on God and the Bible being circulated on the Internet and being received as though they were coming from the fountain of truth. The more sensational these supposed revelations are, the faster they circulate.

In recent times the Jesus Seminar has been something of a sensation. In their quest to find the real Jesus, the participants have determined as of the date of this writing that nearly very little recorded in the Gospels about Christ actually happened. Ellen White gives the following explanation for such misguided views—they do not have the illumination of the Holy Spirit. "It is as true now as in apostolic days, that without the illumination of the divine Spirit, humanity cannot discern the glory of Christ. The truth and the work of God are unappreciated by a world-loving and compromising Christianity. Not in the ways of ease, of earthly honor or worldly conformity, are the followers of the Master found. They are far in advance, in the paths of toil, and humiliation, and reproach, in the front of the battle 'against the principalities, against the powers, against the world rulers of this darkness, against the spiritual hosts of wickedness in the heavenly places.' Eph. 6:12, R. V." (*The Desire of Ages*, 508, 509).

Nevertheless, as we study the way God has preserved and presented His Word to us, we find that the Bible:

1. Is trustworthy (2 Peter1:19)

2. Is written without bias in exact fidelity (4T:9; 370)

3. Even its science is authentic (*Fundamentals of Christian Education*, 84, 85)

Therefore, distortions do not come from the inspired prophets who were directed in their writings by the Holy Spirit. Such distortions would have to come from later translators, copyists, and particularly from contemporary interpreters who are prone to distort Bible truths because of erroneous presuppositions.

Need Right Attitudes and Presuppositions

"Rightly dividing" (2 Tim. 2:15) the Word means approaching it with right attitudes and preconceptions consistent with the nature of the Bible as the trustworthy and inspired revelation of God's will.

"God will have a people upon the earth to maintain the Bible, and the Bible only, as the standard of all doctrines and the basis of all reforms. The opinions of learned men, the deductions of science, the creeds or decisions of ecclesiastical councils, as numerous and discordant as are the churches which they represent, the voice of the majority—not one nor all of these should be regarded as evidence for or against any point of religious faith. Before accepting any doctrine or precept, we should demand a plain 'Thus saith the Lord' in its support.

"Satan is constantly endeavoring to attract attention to man in the place of God. He leads the people to look to bishops, to pastors, to professors of theology, as their guides, instead of searching the Scriptures to learn their duty for themselves. Then, by controlling the minds of these leaders, he can influence the multitudes according to his will" (*The Great Controversy*, 595).

Even humble people who seek the guidance of the Holy Spirit can lead souls to the Christ of the Bible. On a Sunday in January many years ago, a teenager plodded through a blinding snowfall on his way to church. It was bitterly cold—actually too cold for him to be out, but this English boy felt a deep need to meet with Christians although he had never given his life to God. He turned down a narrow lane and stumbled into a Methodist chapel. Only thirteen souls, including himself, had braved the weather.

Eleven o'clock came and went. The minister did not show up. Finally a deacon leafed hurriedly through his Bible, found a text, and made his way up to the pulpit. He was not a preacher, but it was his duty to do the best he could.

The text he chose was Isaiah 45:22: "Look unto me, and be ye saved, all the ends of the earth: for I am God, and there is none else." He began discussing what he saw in the text, but in about ten minutes he had said about everything he could think of. He was about to offer the benediction when he noticed the unhappy-looking boy sitting shivering in the back row. "Young man," the deacon called out, "you look miserable this morning. You need to look to Jesus and be saved. Young man, look to Jesus!"

The Spirit used that humble preacher in a mighty way to reach a cold heart in a cold church. That boy did look to Jesus. His name was Charles Haddon Spurgeon, and he lived to become one of the greatest preachers of his time.

The Thrill of Personal Discovery

All can share the thrill and joy of biblical discovery. Often we hear it repeated that the Bible is an inexhaustible treasure chest overflowing with glorious gems of truth. However, most people who study the Bible seem content merely to glance briefly across the picked-over surface of this treasure without ever becoming fully aware of the excitement and pleasure that comes from personal discovery of gems hidden beneath.

In His parable recorded in Matthew 13:44, Christ likens the "kingdom of heaven" to a treasure hid in a field. We mentioned this parable in chapter 2. But because some of the parables are likely subjects for using our imagination, let's add to our previous discussion some points of interest, being careful not in any way to violate what Christ had in mind as He told the story. A man is working his neighbor's field on shares. He doesn't have and can't afford land of his own. One day as he is plowing the field, the plow strikes something hard and metallic. He stops the oxen and quickly gets down on his hands and knees and scoops up the dirt. In a few moments he has uncovered a small treasure chest and, as he breaks it open, he recognizes that it contains a fortune in coins and jewels. Quickly he covers it up, marking the spot, and runs over to his neighbor's house.

"Neighbor," he says, trying to hide his excitement, "I would like to buy your field. How much will you take for it?"

"I'm sorry, friend. It is not for sale. This property has been in my family for generations, and I don't want to sell it."

But the man insists and persists until finally the neighbor, in order to get rid of him, places a ridiculously high price on the field.

"All right, I'll buy it! Give me until three o'clock this afternoon to raise the money."

Quickly he runs home and begins taking stock of all his resources. Naturally, he doesn't have enough. Immediately this man, who must buy the field to own its treasure, begins selling his furniture. He's in such a rush that he has no time to explain to his wife what he's doing. Soon the furniture is gone, and still he's far short. He remembers a friend who has been wanting to buy his house; and because he is willing to settle for a fraction of its worth, the friend is able to pay him cash. Still there isn't enough! He goes back and strips the house, even selling every bit of clothing except for that which he and his family are wearing. His wife's precious dowry goes. She is terribly upset, but he has no time to argue with her. Still there is more to raise. Without a moment's hesitation, he borrows the remaining amount at a usurious rate of interest, promising to sell himself and his family into slavery if he cannot make the payments.

Finally he has enough, and it's almost three o'clock. Without a word of explanation to anyone, he races back to his neighbor's house and completes the transaction for the field. By now his wife has gathered her parents and her in-laws and several of her close friends. They are weeping and wailing, for they are sure the husband has gone stark, raving mad. They follow him at a safe distance as he races back to the field. Now they're certain of his insanity as they see him get down on his hands and knees and begin to paw up the earth. But in just a few moments their mourning turns to shouts of rejoicing as he presents them with his newfound treasure, now theirs to keep.

It is important to look for the main point or points in interpreting a parable. The point Jesus' story makes is that when we find hidden treasure worth far more than anything we ever expected to find or own, we joyfully give all that we have for it. Tremendous joy comes in discovering the hidden treasures of the Word of God. The reward we receive is worth far more than the effort it takes to discover it. And the effort itself becomes joyful, just as with the man in the parable who became so thrilled that he joyfully sold all that he had. The effort and trouble that it took to sell his things quickly, even at a loss, was no bother to him but was exciting in itself as he anticipated the final results.

In the light of the fact that the joy and thrill of discovery are so rewarding, why is the search for the jewels of truth to be found in the Bible treasure chest so neglected? Because work is involved. Anything worthwhile takes effort, of course. And how much we miss if we are unwilling to put forth the effort!

A truly stupendous privilege is involved—the privilege of sharing God's truth as He reveals it to us in a way as meaningful as if the words recorded hundreds and even thousands of years ago had been placed in the Scriptures and preserved for just this one moment of time—the thrilling moment of personal discovery.

Naturally, we cannot fairly expect the deepest and most satisfying discoveries at first or all at once. Even after the thrill of discovering the Messiah, it took the disciples quite awhile to recognize how unique and precious this discovery really was. Likewise, it takes training, experience, and discipline to discover and recognize Bible truth for yourself. But the results are sure. God Himself guarantees this in His promise "And ye shall seek me, and find me, when ye shall search for me with all your heart" (Jeremiah 29:13).

Daniel 12:10 promises that those who study prayerfully and diligently and "shall be purified" WILL be able to understand God's messages. But that is not true of the wicked. "None of the wicked shall understand." Why is a willingness to obey God a prerequisite to receiving light? What purpose would there be in pouring out truth to those who have no intention of following it. When the Holy Spirit comes into our hearts and lives, He guides us into all truth (John 16:13).

How Jesus Dealt With Those Who Were Not Honest in Their Approach to Bible Study

"The Pharisees built the tombs of the prophets, and adorned their sepulchers, and said one to another, If we had lived in the days of our fathers, we would not have united with them in shedding the blood of God's servants. At the same time they were planning to take the life of His Son. This should be a lesson to us. It should open our eyes to the power of Satan to deceive the mind that turns from the light of truth. Many follow in the track of the Pharisees. They revere those who have died for their faith. They wonder at the blindness of the Jews in rejecting Christ. Had we lived in His day, they declare, we would gladly have received His teaching; we would never have been partakers in the guilt of those who rejected the Saviour. But when obedience to God requires self-denial and humiliation, these very persons stifle their convictions, and refuse obedience. . . .

"Looking forward, Jesus declared that the impenitence of the Jews and their intolerance of God's servants would be the same in the future as it had been in the past:

" 'Wherefore, behold, I send unto you prophets, and wise men, and scribes: and some of them ye shall kill and crucify; and some of them shall ye scourge in your synagogues, and persecute them from city to city.' Prophets and wise men, full of faith and the Holy Ghost,—Stephen, James, and many others,— would be condemned and slain. With hand uplifted to heaven, and a divine light enshrouding His person, Christ spoke as a judge to those before Him. His voice, that had so often been heard in gentleness and entreaty, was now heard in rebuke and condemnation. The listeners shuddered. Never was the impression made by His words and His look to be effaced.

"Christ's indignation was directed against the hypocrisy, the gross sins, by which men were destroying their own souls, deceiving the people and dishonoring God. In the specious deceptive reasoning of the priests and rulers He discerned the working of satanic agencies. Keen and searching had been His denunciation of sin; but He spoke no words of retaliation. . . . So the Christian who lives in harmony with God, possessing the sweet attributes of love and mercy, will feel a righteous indignation against sin; but he will not be roused by passion to revile those who revile him" (*The Desire of Ages*, 618-620).

Chapter 12

THE GREAT CONTROVERSY THEME

None of us asked for the privilege, but whether we like it or not, all of us are at center stage in the great drama of the universe. By reason of being born when we were and where we are, all humanity is now caught up in the great controversy between Christ and Satan regarding the character of God, His law, and His sovereignty over the universe. This conflict originated in heaven when a created being, endowed with freedom of choice, because of self-exaltation became Satan, God's adversary, and led a portion of the angels into rebellion. Later, he led Adam and Eve into sin, thus introducing the spirit of rebellion into this world. Sin resulted in the distortion of the image of God in humanity, the disordering of the created world, and its eventual devastation at the time of the worldwide flood. Under the observation of the entire universe, this world became the arena of the universal conflict out of which the God of love will ultimately be vindicated.

But we humans are not in this alone. All heaven is committed to helping us. To assist His people in this controversy, Christ sends the Holy Spirit and the loyal angels to guide, protect, and sustain us in the way of salvation (Adapted from SDA Fundamental Belief, no. 8).

Because sin and its effects still exist on earth, we often

are reminded of its terrible results. Rise (Ree-seh) Colson came as a breath of fresh air to the little group of believers attempting to establish a church in Harrison, Tennessee. Although a theology graduate from Southwestern Adventist College, she was working as a nurse. But her heart was in becoming a Seventh-day Adventist minister. Not being able to find a position upon graduation, she moved to the Chattanooga area to be near relatives. She was thrilled to find a little church that needed her talents and threw herself unreservedly into helping it develop.

Rise preached, gave Bible studies, and had a special burden for ministering to the homeless. But one form of ministry in which she engaged bothered her fellow church members. She picked up hitchhikers, often bringing them to church and evangelistic meetings. Our concern was that we did not feel it safe for a young woman to pick up hitchhikers.

On August 2, 1995, on her way to work near Knoxville, she picked up her last hitchhiker. Her body was found two days later when someone spotted her little white pickup truck near an abandoned building and found her bruised and mutilated body nearby.

Passersby had seen a man beating a woman and kicking her near a white pickup. One motorist even stopped his car and ran back to help Rise but later told police the man forced the woman back into the truck and sped away. The motorist followed the truck but lost it in the traffic. Police finally picked up a drifter hitchhiking on I-75 who admitted he had killed Rise. He reportedly told the police that he became angry when she would not turn off the religious tape she was playing and became even more furious when she kept "preaching at him."

The little church at Harrison experienced tremendous shock when they met on Sabbath, the day after Rise's body had been found and identified, and many of them learned for the first time about the gruesome murder. Why had the Lord allowed such a horrible death to come on the woman who was contributing so much to the growth of the church? One blessing came out of this terrible tragedy. It drew the church closer together as a family and made them more determined than ever to thwart the purposes of the enemy of souls who had shown such intense hatred toward a dedicated servant of God.

Most people when they have bitter experiences question why a good God created a bad world. He didn't! What happened? The inevitable. After the Creator brought ten thousand times ten thousand and thousands of thousands of thinking beings into existence, all having the power of choice, someone somewhere would surely misuse that power. Surprisingly, but perhaps not so surprisingly, the being that misused this God-given power turned out to be Lucifer, the highest and most talented of all created beings.

"Lucifer in heaven, before his rebellion, was a high and exalted angel, next in honor to God's own Son. . . . His form was perfect: his bearing noble and majestic. A special light beamed in his countenance and shone around him brighter and more beautiful than around the other angels: yet Christ, God's dear Son, had the pre-eminence over all the angelic host. He was one with the Father before the angels were created. Lucifer was envious of Christ, and gradually assumed command which devolved on Christ alone" (*The Story of Redemption,* 13).

Lucifer should have recognized that, as a created being, he had no right to the respect and worship accorded deity. But instead he harbored jealous thoughts and confided them to his angel companions, proposing questions that were designed to sow seeds of dissatisfaction. Lucifer's subtle insinuations resulted in one-third of the angels committing themselves to his side. Misled by his beguiling lies, they felt that he could set up a government superior to God's. With infinite patience their Creator attempted to explain His actions—to persuade the rebel and his sympathizers to abandon the disastrous course they were following. He attempted to make clear that heaven's laws, grounded in love, were essential to happiness. But when Lucifer and his fellow rebels refused to accept explanations or to respond to entreaties, God had no recourse but to cast them out of heaven.

Even then God did not at once destroy Lucifer and his followers. He gave them time and opportunity to see that their charges against His character and law were unjustified.

God warned Adam and Eve in the Garden of Eden that the natural consequence of disobedience would be death. Lucifer, who had become Satan, saw this as an opportunity to entice the first humans to eat the forbidden fruit and join him in rebellion. Tragically and incredibly, Adam and Eve yielded to Satan's temptation.

Heaven Provided a Saviour

Even after they sinned, God in His mercy spared the first couples' lives in order that the guilty pair still might have opportunity to repent. However, the penalty for breaking God's law had to be met, and the members of the Godhead with divine insight previously had made provision for this. Long before the great rebellion, they had agreed that God the Son, whom we know as Jesus, would come to this earth and die for sin, taking the place of sinners. How easy it is to mention what Jesus did without understanding fully all that it means!

We can show our appreciation for what Christ has done for us by giving our hearts as monuments dedicated to the Lamb of God who was willing to come to die in our stead.

The decision by the Council of Heaven for Jesus to die for us was made before sin entered the universe. After the Fall, the effects of sin became more and more evident—not only in the human race but in all of nature. The principles advocated by Satan, at first but dimly seen as dangerous, bore a harvest of evil fruit. Nineteen centuries ago, when Christ was murdered because of our transgression, the inhabitants of heaven and the other worlds saw clearly the horrible nature of sin. Then they realized how right God was and how wrong Satan was.

After a few years of struggling to bring Israel into a right relationship to the kingdom of God, Jesus set His face steadfastly to go to Jerusalem, suffering, and death. His blood drenched the cross, but today that cross unites people of all races, cultures, and status in life under one glorious title—Christian. That precious blood also demonstrated to the universe the horrible nature of sin and the true character of Satan's rebellion.

When Jesus died, the citizens of heaven and the unfallen worlds recognized for a certainty that God is love and that His law is just and necessary. But to give the citizens of our world ample opportunity to understand the issues in the great controversy between Christ and Satan and to allow the people perfect freedom to choose whose side they wanted to join, God permitted the sin drama to play itself out in this world.

Today the conflict is nearing its close. With great urgency the Holy Spirit and the angels of heaven are seeking to help people choose God's side—to put loyalty to God, righteousness, and truth above even life itself. To assist His people in this controversy, Christ sends the Holy Spirit and the loyal angels to guide, protect, and sustain them in the way of salvation. The Bible makes it clear that the ultimate outcome will be complete victory for God and the vindication of His character and law.

The basketball team could not practice in their own gym because a special program was being held there. Instead, they were using another high school's gym. As the players raced up and down the court, an old janitor sat in the stands, waiting for the team to finish so he could get to work. While he waited, he read.

During a short rest period one of the players came up to the janitor and asked what he was reading. "I'm reading the Bible, the book of Revelation," he answered.

The young man leaned over and glimpsed a few words such as "Alpha," "Omega," and "Sardis." "Do you really understand all that stuff?" he asked.

The janitor smiled. "Sure I do. It says Jesus wins!"

Jesus has already won. But until that glorious day when He returns to put an end to all sin, good and evil will continue side by side. Today supernatural forces are continuing the deadly warfare begun long ago in heaven. Planet Earth is the battlefield. But only a short time remains until Christ comes to claim the victory He won on the cross so long ago.

Why Did Jesus Come?

The basic question answered by the Bible worldview outlined briefly above is: Why did Jesus come to this planet? Seventh-day Adventists believe that the Cross of Christ has universal, as well as local planet, significance. Jesus came to live and die for more than our salvation. Much more was at stake. He came to answer a charge against the justice of God that preceded our human need for salvation. Satan's mysterious rebellion took place before this world existed. After Creation, Satan claimed that it is impossible for created human beings to keep God's law. This is one of the reasons why the member of the Godhead we know as Jesus became a human being. Jesus demonstrated that human beings *can* keep the law of God and gain the victory over sin.

In order to demonstrate the possibility of our living sin-free lives by allowing Jesus to gain the victory over sin in us, Christ had to come to this world and live here as a human being—not as a God. Satan had no quarrel with the fact that God could keep His own law. He focused on convincing people that it was impossible for created beings to do so. For the purpose of proving Satan wrong, Jesus lived as a man—emptying Himself of the use of His divine powers while here on earth yet remaining divine. (See Phil. 2:5-7.) He was fully God on earth, but He lived as a dependent human being, clinging to His Father. This is why He called Himself the "true vine" (John 15:1). The glorious news of the everlasting gospel is that what Jesus did, by His grace and the Spirit's power, we can do too.

In recent years the idea that I term *impossibility thinking* has crept into the church. It's the belief that we cannot live as Jesus called us to live when He invited us to take up the cross of self-denial and FOLLOW Him. We should not be surprised by Satan's attempt to discourage us in the last moments of time in order to delay Christ's second coming. Ever since Eden he has done all he could to convince humans that it is impossible to keep God's laws.

What we need is a new infusion of "possibility thinking"—a realization of all that God promises and makes possible for His people. That which so many claim is impossible, we not only can but must accomplish by His grace.

We Dare Not Be Indifferent

Seventh-day Adventists believe that the created beings from the unfallen populated planets, along with heaven's unfallen angels, watched with intense interest as Jesus came to earth. (See *The Great Controversy*, 503.) They, too, had a stake in His life and death. In Jesus, as a created human, God would demonstrate to the universe that He is just and that Satan's charge of injustice is false.

Yet so many seem indifferent to these great issues in which the entire universe is caught up. Some years ago I read that in London there is a statue of Christ bearing His cross. It is said that thousands of people pass by each day without even noticing it. An inscription under the statue reads: "Is it nothing to all ye that pass by?" Jesus gladly took up the cross for each of us. What does that mean to us? Are we willing to bear the cross of self-denial for Him?

Christ's victory at the cross had universal significance. Now it could be seen by all created beings that God was just in removing sin from the universe. A long time ago, a snake confused a perfect woman who lived in a perfect garden. The issue was that of the nature of sin. Satan still tries to perplex us regarding the basic issues involved in the great controversy that is going on for our souls. Too often, he is successful.

Burt Hunter, a reporter-photographer in Long Beach, California, found himself on a strange mission one foggy morning. He was to interview and take pictures of a woman snake charmer.

When Burt rang the doorbell at an impressive mansion, he was surprised at the beauty of the woman who answered. She didn't look like a snake charmer. He blurted out, "I don't understand why a wealthy, attractive woman such as yourself is engaged in this kind of business."

The lady smiled as she replied, "Oh, I don't do it because I have to. It's a fascinating hobby. I like the element of danger involved. Someday soon I plan to give it up and spend more time with my flowers. I can quit this any time I want to."

As Burt set up his equipment, the woman brought in baskets containing the cobras. She confidently lifted out some of the deadly snakes as he snapped pictures of her handling them. Then she cautioned, "Be especially quiet now and don't make any quick moves. I'm going to take out my newest snake. It isn't completely used to me yet."

Suddenly she stiffened, whispering to the photographer, "Something's wrong. I'm going to have to put him back." She opened the basket slowly and began to lower the snake into it. As Burt watched, fascinated, there was a lightning-jab of the cobra's head as it buried it's fangs in her wrist.

Forcing the snake down and securing the basket, the woman clutched her arm. She spoke quietly to Burt, "Go quickly to my medicine chest and bring the snake serum. Hurry!"

Trembling, Burt returned with the precious vial. She instructed him to take out the syringe and fit the needle on. Then she told him how to withdraw the serum. Burt struggled with the unfamiliar task, his hands shaking. He braced his arm against the table as he tried desperately to get the needle into the vial. Suddenly he gasped. His clumsy fingers had crushed the tiny bottle. The serum, now useless, dripped through his fingers.

"Tell me," he urged. "Where can I get another?"

In a quiet voice she responded, "That was my last one."

Her agony soon ended, but Burt's lived on to embitter the rest of his life. Often he thought of her statement, "I can quit this any time I want to." (Adapted from Marjorie Grant Burns, "Broken!" *The Youth's Instructor*, 25 Dec. 1951, 5, 6, 18, 19).

Many today who, following Mother Eve's example, play with the deadly serpents of sin feel that somehow it won't hurt them. But soon the vial that contains the only remedy for sin will not be available. We must be willing to accept the provision that Heaven made so long ago to provide us a Saviour from sin now, before it is too late.

Although Satan lost the universe as a result of his attacks on Christ at Jesus' first coming, he has thrown superhuman effort into a wild last-day attack upon the remnant church (Rev. 12:17). He has learned through history that his most effective means is to attack from within rather than from without. Isn't that why we see so many different groups *within* the church attacking the church on so many issues?

In our approach to studying the Word of God we need to keep this great controversy theme in mind in order to provide the overall framework we need. But this framework must of necessity include only what the Scriptures reveal rather than becoming a human concept imposed on the Bible. "The Bible is its own expositor. Scripture is to be compared with scripture. The student should learn to view the word as a whole, and to see the relation of its parts. He should gain a knowledge of its grand central theme, of God's original purpose for the world, of the rise of the great controversy, and of the work of redemption. He should understand the nature of the two principles that are contending for supremacy, and should learn to trace their working through the records of history and prophecy, to the great consummation. He should see how this controversy enters into every phase of human experience; how in every act of life he himself reveals the one or the other of the two antagonistic motives; and how, whether he will or not, he is even now deciding upon which side of the controversy he will be found" (*Education*, 190).

How We, Like Christ, Can Meet Satan's Attacks and Overcome Sin

"Jesus met Satan with the words of Scripture. 'It is written,' He said. In every temptation the weapon of His warfare was the word of God. Satan demanded of Christ a miracle as a sign of His divinity. But that which is greater than all miracles, a firm reliance upon a 'Thus saith the Lord,' was a sign that could not be controverted. So long as Christ held to this position, the tempter could gain no advantage.

"It was in the time of greatest weakness that Christ was assailed by the fiercest temptations. . . . Satan has taken advantage of the weakness of humanity. And he will still work in the same way. Whenever one is encompassed with clouds, perplexed by circumstances, or afflicted by poverty or distress, Satan is at hand to tempt and annoy. . . . If we would meet him as Jesus did, we should escape many a defeat. By parleying with the enemy, we give him an advantage. . . .

"In the last great conflict of the controversy with Satan those who are loyal to God will see every earthly support cut off. Because they refuse to break His law in obedience to earthly powers, they will be forbidden to buy or sell. It will finally be decreed that they shall be put to death. See Rev. 13:11-17. But to the obedient is given the promise, 'He shall dwell on high: his place of defense shall be the munitions of rocks: bread shall be given him; his waters shall be sure.' Isa. 33:16. By this promise the children of God will live. When the earth shall be wasted with famine, they shall be fed. . . .

"In our own strength it is impossible for us to deny the clamors of our fallen nature. Through this channel Satan will bring temptation upon us. Christ knew that the enemy would come to every human being, to take advantage of hereditary weakness, and by his false insinuations to ensnare all whose trust is not in God. And by passing over the ground which man must travel, our Lord has prepared the way for us to overcome. It is not His will that we should be placed at a disadvantage in the conflict with Satan. . . .

" 'The prince of this world cometh,' said Jesus, 'and hath nothing in Me.'

John 14:30. There was in Him nothing that responded to Satan's sophistry. He did not consent to sin. Not even by a thought did He yield to temptation. **So it may be with us.** Christ's humanity was united with divinity; He was fitted for the conflict by the indwelling of the Holy Spirit. And He came to make us partakers of the divine nature. So long as we are united to Him by faith, sin has no more dominion over us. God reaches for the hand of faith in us to direct it to lay fast hold upon the divinity of Christ, that we may attain to perfection of character.

"And how this is accomplished, Christ has shown us. By what means did He overcome in the conflict with Satan? By the word of God. Only by the word could He resist temptation. 'It is written,' He said. And unto us are given 'exceeding great and precious promises: that by these ye might be partakers of the divine nature, having escaped the corruption that is in the world through lust.' 2 Peter 1:4. Every promise in God's word is ours. 'By every word that proceedeth out of the mouth of God' are we to live. When assailed by temptation, look not to circumstances or to the weakness of self, but to the power of the word. All its strength is yours. 'Thy word,' says the psalmist, 'have I hid in mine heart, that I might not sin against Thee.' Ps. 119:11" (*The Desire of Ages*, 121-123).

Chapter 13

THE ADVENTIST REVOLUTION OVER REVELATION

If an Adventist who died soon after Ellen White's time were to be raised from his grave to see what was happening to the church today, he would be impressed with our numbers and statistics: nearly 10 million members—the majority in the Third World; a growing number of respected universities, hospitals, and publishing houses; Global Missions and Adventist Frontier Missions, along with Student Missionary and Maranatha projects, on the cutting edge of the modern missionary movement.

But then he reads a few popular Adventist books, listens to some Sabbath morning sermons, and visits with some of our more liberal teachers. It wouldn't be long before his hair would be standing on end. This visitor from the early years of the century would find some Adventists advocating a new ecumenism based on charismatic renewal and gradually would discover that nearly every Adventist doctrine, from inspiration to the Second Coming, is under attack. Last-day events as outlined in *The Great Controversy* are considered outdated. Sunday laws are considered remote. While some in the scientific world are calling Darwin into question, he would find a group of Adventist scholars accepting the basic premises of evolution. The Spirit of Prophecy is considered irrelevant in certain church circles, and, strangely, in a time when the Seventh-day Adventist lifestyle is gaining acceptance from the scientific world, some Adventists are not paying much attention to the life-saving principles God has outlined.

Throughout our history Adventists have argued over a variety of theological issues but have considered the Bible the final authority. The member brought from the turn-of-the-century church would find that some modern Adventists disagree with the concept that the Bible is inspired and trustworthy, challenging the position that our only safety is in accepting it as the rule of faith and practice.

However, he would be encouraged to learn that the majority of church members are conservative. Even those who welcome liberal teachings that give them a rationale for continuing to sin have a nagging feeling that breaking the commandments is NOT the fruit of righteousness.

What is happening in the Adventist Church reflects the significant realignment taking place in most churches and many religions today. In some ways the split between conservatives and liberals creates camps of thought that are more diametrically opposed to each other than are the traditional theological divisions that separate denominations. A subtle emphasis on pluralism in our standards and beliefs is dividing our church into two camps that will culminate in a great churchquake. Then many who have shifted from belief in the Bible as the trustworthy revelation of God's will in order to accommodate themselves to current liberal trends will learn too late that they have made the wrong choice. To Adventists who believe that the final division in the Christian world will be between two camps, characterized on one hand by the full acceptance of biblical authority and, on the other, by a great ecumenical pluralism, the current division comes as the expected rather than the unexpected.

In the August 11, 1997, issue of *Christianity Today,*

James Edwards, who is part of a group of pastors and lay leaders intent on keeping the Presbyterian Church (USA) from drifting into secularism and acculturation of the gospel, states: "As a member of the team that drafted the 1991 minority report in opposition to the massive majority report (*Keeping Body and Soul Together*), I can attest to the virtual silence—or opposition—of seminary faculties, religion departments of denominational colleges, and church bureaucrats on the question of defending biblical theology and morality against its capitulation to moral norms. . . . My experience in the Presbyterian church has caused me to see in Scripture what I had never seen before, obvious as it is. The chief threat to the Word of God and to the people of God . . . come[s] not from without but from within. . . . The gospel is not entrusted to the church to refashion in each generation. It is rather the church that is entrusted to the gospel, to obey from its heart the rule of faith to which it is handed over" ("At the Crossroads," *Christianity Today*, 1 Aug. 1997, 25).

The 1995 General Conference study paper on "The Authority of Scripture" indicates the extent of this inspiration/revelation issue in the Adventist Church: "Contemporary theology of almost any shade is now in crisis. It has become relativistic and hesitating. There is no lack of religious literature, to be sure, but one scarcely hears a sure word that recognizes divine authority. The foundations have been shaken. The major cause of this ferment is as plain as the fact itself: An increasing number of our contemporaries deny the existence of a solid platform on which Christian thinking can be built.

"The breach between the Reformation and the Roman Catholic Church, 450 years ago, is narrow when compared with the chasm separating those who affirm and those who deny the existence of an objective divine revelation. In those days each side acknowledged the existence of revealed truth. They differed only in its interpretation. Today there is a widespread skepticism as to whether an objective revelation exists at all.

"General denial that divine revelation is objectively communicated in historical occurrences and intelligible statements of truth has proved to be destructive for theology. In the present climate, the Bible provides themes for theology, but no norms. . . . The Bible student is free to bend revealed facts to his or her liking and to relativize the biblical truth, dissolving the biblical message in the acid of human subjectivity.

"Such trends have not left Seventh-day Adventists unaffected. Today, in place of the time-honored view that Scripture is 'the infallible revelation of His [God's] will,' 'the authoritative revealer of doctrines, and the trustworthy record of God's acts in history' (Fundamental Beliefs, no. 1), some among us have come to claim that the truth of revelation is so wholly other, so far beyond comprehension that no one can really say what it is or what it is not. Christian truths, we are told, are relative rather than absolute and therefore neither universal or normative.

"Others no longer seem determined to limit themselves to Scripture in the formulation of their views. Various sources—including Scripture, to be sure—are supposed to contribute information from which theological statements are compiled. What happens in fact is that *one* source comes to be treated as the preferred final authority. It may be reason, science, experience, or some other factor, but is not often Scripture."

Warning Given Against False Views of Inspiration

Many years ago God warned Adventists that: "In our day, as of old, the vital truths of God's word are set aside for human theories and speculations. Many professed ministers of the gospel do not accept the whole Bible as the inspired word. One wise man rejects one portion; another questions another part. They set up their judgment as superior to the word; and the Scripture which they do teach rests upon their own authority. Its divine authenticity is destroyed. Thus the seeds of infidelity are sown broadcast; for the people become confused and know not what to believe. There are many beliefs that the mind has no right to entertain. In the days of Christ the rabbis put a forced, mystical construction upon many portions of Scripture. Because the plain teaching of God's word condemned their practices, they tried to destroy its force. The same thing is done today. The word of God is made to appear mysterious and obscure in order to excuse transgression of His law. Christ rebuked these practices in His day. He taught that the word of God was to be understood by all. He pointed to the Scriptures as of unquestionable authority, and we should do the same. The Bible is to be presented as the word of the infinite God, as the end of all controversy and the foundation of all faith" (*Christ's Object Lessons,* 39).

Added to this is God's challenge to church leaders: "God has a special work for the men of experience to do. They are to guard the cause of God. They are to see that the work of God is not committed to men who feel it their privilege to move out on their own independent judgment, to preach whatever they please, and to be responsible to no one for their instructions or work. Let this spirit of self-sufficiency once rule in our midst, and there will be no harmony of action, no unity of spirit, no safety for the work, and no healthful growth in the cause. There will be false teachers, evil workers, who will, by insinuating error, draw away souls from the truth. Christ prayed that His followers might be one as He and the Father were one. Those who desire to see this prayer answered, should seek to discourage the slightest tendency to division, and try to keep the spirit of unity and love among brethren" (*Review and Herald,* 29 May 1888).

Samuel Koranteng-Pipim notices the strange phenomena that has come into the Adventist Church as a result of not taking seriously the warnings given above. "There was a time when Adventists were known as the 'People of the Book,' even 'Bookworms'! In our day, however, we have become 'tapeworms,' chasing the latest audio and video tapes from our self-appointed authorities, be they pastors, professors of theology and science, psychologists, parents, or personal acquaintances. But we are to receive the Word, 'not as the word of men, but as it is in truth, the word of God, which effectually worketh also in you who believe' (1 Thess. 2:13).

"This means that rather than holding up human traditions, opinion polls, subjective experience, the pronouncements of learned men, and the latest research findings in naturalistic science and secular psychology as alternative sources of dependable knowledge, we must always insist upon the Bible and the Bible only as the rule of faith and lifestyle" (*Receiving the Word* [Berrien Springs, Mich.: Berean Books, 1996], 329).

The Revelation Revolution Will NOT Succeed

One of the major reasons for Adventist members to become more than familiar with the Bible at this time is to be able to distinguish clearly between the false and the true. Here in the last moments of time we're being besieged on every side by insidious teachings.

For decades the Western world has been so wrapped in the stifling cocoon of technology that religion has been all but excluded from everyday life and thought. Because of the tremendous promise of scientific advance, a large number of people decided they didn't need God or the hope of a future heaven. Why, heaven was to be established on earth right now! Then technology seemed to turn on us. Nuclear weapons, environmental pollution, and cancer-producing agents in so many things have pulled out our props and left us with uncertainty and fear.

Because the old values largely have been thrown away, modern men and women have been left with no place to turn; and the devil—actually a large number of devils—fills the vacuum. This is evident in the current popularity of the occult, astrology, oriental mysticism, and the rise of cults. We are surrounded by a growing bombardment of daily satanic lies. The only way to avoid the devil's last-day deceptions is to prevent *truth* decay.

It is truer than it ever has been that we need to search the Scriptures daily, that we may know the way of the Lord, and that we not "be deceived by religious fallacies. The world is full of false theories and seductive spiritualistic ideas, which tend to destroy clear spiritual perception, and to lead away from truth and holiness. Especially at this time, we need to heed the warning, 'Let no man deceive you with vain words' (Eph. 5:6)" (Ellen White, *Selected Messages,* 1:170).

There is another tragedy in the church today. Even among those Adventists who, without question, receive the Bible "as it is in truth, the word of God" (1 Thess. 2:13). Many neglect to follow the example of the Thessalonians and give the Word of God a chance to work "effectually" in them.

But no matter how much you come to enjoy Bible study, unless it brings about a change in your thinking and in your pattern of living, it has not accomplished what God intends it to. However, if you faithfully apply yourself to careful study, you certainly can expect the fulfillment of the promise that "he who opens the Scriptures, and feeds upon the heavenly manna, becomes a partaker of the divine nature" (Ellen White, *Review and*

Herald, 28 June 1892).

Only need-motivated and God-directed Bible study brings us God's words—words to live and grow by. Words that will enable us to overcome the divisions Satan is attempting to bring into the Adventist Church.

We don't want division but it will come. "Division will come in the church. Two parties will be developed. The wheat and the tares grow up together for the harvest" (*Selected Messages*, 2:114). The divisions now developing in the church indicate that "We are in the shaking time, the time when everything that can be shaken will be shaken. The Lord will not excuse those who know the truth if they do not in word and deed obey His commands" (*Testimonies for the Church*, 6:332).

How many will be affected? "When the law of God is made void the church will be sifted by fiery trials, and a larger proportion than we now anticipate will give heed to seducing spirits and doctrines of devils" (*Selected Messages*, 2:174).

Who will be shaken out? "Those who have had privileges and opportunities to become intelligent in regard to the truth and yet who continue to counterwork the work God would have accomplished will be purged out, for God accepts the service of no man whose interest is divided" (*Last Day Events*, 175).

"The church may appear as about to fall, but it does not fall. It remains, while the sinners in Zion will be sifted out—the chaff separated from the precious wheat. This is a terrible ordeal, but nevertheless it must take place" (*Selected Messages*, 2:380).

Even though it seems to some that the remnant church is about to fall apart, it won't happen that way. A victorious, triumphant church will rise out of its present crisis of confidence and will be joined by a large number who see Christ's character reproduced in His people. These gladly join the worldwide call to come out of Babylon and not suffer her plagues.

How Jesus Deals With Those Who Reject Light

"Those who shall be overcomers are to be highly exalted before God and before his angels. Christ has promised that he will confess their names before his Father and before the holy angels of heaven. He has given us abundant promises to encourage us to be overcomers. The True Witness has given us the assurance that he has set before us an open door, which no man can shut. Those who are seeking to be faithful to God may be denied many of the privileges of the world; their way may be hedged up and their work hindered by the enemies of truth; but there is no power that can close the door of communication between God and their souls. The Christian himself may close this door by indulgence in sin, or by rejection of heaven's light. He may turn away his ears from hearing the message of truth, and in this way sever the connection between God and his soul.

"You may have ears, and not hear. You may have eyes, and not see the light, nor receive the illumination that God has provided for you. You may close the door to light as effectually as the Pharisees closed the door to Christ when he taught among them. They would not receive the light and knowledge he brought, because it did not come in the way they had expected it to come. Christ was the light of the world, and if they had received the light he graciously brought to them, it would have resulted in their salvation, but they rejected the Holy One of Israel. Christ said of them that they loved darkness rather than light, because their deeds were evil. For every one that doeth evil hateth the light, neither cometh to the light, lest his deeds should be reproved." He said, "Ye will not come to me, that ye might have life." The way was open; but by their own course of action they closed the door, and severed their connection with Christ. We may do the same by rejecting light and truth. . . .

"Every day we have the precious privilege of connecting ourselves with Christ, who has set before us an open door. All heaven is at our command. If we are obedient children of God, we may draw daily supplies of grace. Whatever temptations, trials, or persecutions may come upon us, we need not be discouraged. Neither man nor Satan can close the door which Christ has opened for us. . . .

"We need not look into the future with anxiety; for God has made it possible for us to be overcomers every day, and he will give needed grace, that we may be conquerors. I am glad we have only a day at a time in which to work. We should not undervalue its responsibilities, and devote it to the service of the enemy. We should not spend it in arraying ourselves in fashionable attire, in decorating our homes as if we were to be permanent dwellers upon the earth. We should employ its moments in trading with our intrusted talents, in using our ability to glorify God, instead of glorifying ourselves. Our whole study should be how we may win the approbation of God. If we are doing his will, with an eye single to his glory, we shall be able to say, 'I know that my Redeemer liveth'" (*Review and Herald*, 26 March 1889).